GW00891772

Be Happy
with
Prayer, Meditation and Affirmation

by

Mynavati

Be Happy with Prayer, Meditation and Affirmation

by Mynavati

ISBN : 81-86847-06-5

Publishers : Tiger Moon Productions/Cosmic Power Press
email : cosmic power press@yahoo.co.in

Price : £ 9.99

Dedicated to my Guru
Bhagawan Sri Sathya Sai Baba
and
to all my Teachers,
in particular
Sri H.W.L.Poonja (Papaji)
His Holiness the Seventeenth Gyalwa Karmapa
Tai Situ Pa Rinpoche
Gyaltsop Rinpoche
Ringu Tulku Rinpoche
and
to all the members of my family
especially
my husband Sudevan,
my mum,
late father,
son Craig
and his family,
Karen, Christopher and Lucy
and
to all my friends and fellow journeyers
with whom I have been allowed to share
some of these truths
and
finally to Terry
for patiently and lovingly editing the manuscript.

With gratitude, love and devotion,

Mynavati

Disclaimer

The author and publishers are not responsible for any injury to any person attempting to use the practices and methods described in this book.

The reader is requested to take responsibility for his or her mental and physical health and balance. If in doubt as to whether or not you can safely use the practices and methods described in this book, please consult with a professional.

If you have a history of mental illness, alcohol or drug-abuse, or if you are experiencing depression, suicidal tendencies, sleeplessness or nervous exhaustion, please seek professional and ongoing guidance before attempting any continuous spiritual practices and methods.

Credits

We gratefully acknowledge the publishers of the following sources :

1. Cutting Through Spiritual Materialism by Chogyam Trungpa. ©1973 by Chogyam Trungpa. Reprinted by arrangement with Shambhala Publications, Inc., Boston, www.Shambala.com, USA.

2. God Lived With Them by Swami Chetanananda, Aidvaita Ashrama, Mayavati, Himalayas, India, 1997.

3. Sathya Sai Speaks Series, Discourses by Bhagawan Sri Sathya Sai Baba vol. I – XXX, Sri Sathya Sai Books & Publications Trust, Prasanthi Nilayam, A.P., India.

4. Scientific Healing Affirmations by Paramahansa Yogananda, Self-Realization Fellowship, California, USA, 1981.

5. Songs of Enlightenment — Poems by Swami Rama Tirtha, translated from the Urdu and Persian by A.J. Alston, published by Shanti Sadan, London. www.shantisadan.org

6. The Collected Works of St.Teresa of Avila, vol. 1, translated by Kieren Kavanagh, OCD and Otilio Rodriguez OCD, copyright © 1976, revised 1987, Washington Province of Discalced Carmelite Friars, Inc., ICS Publications, 2131 Lincoln Road, N.E. Washington, DC 20002 USA www.icspublications.org

7. The Supreme Yoga, A New Translation of the Yoga Vasishta, v. II, translated by Swami Venkatesananda, by The Divine Life Society, U.P. Himalayas, India, 1995.

8. The Tibetan Book of Living and Dying by Sogyal Rinpoche published by Rider. Used by permission of The Random House Group, Limited.

Suggested Reading

1. Hands of Light : A Guide to Healing through the Human Energy Field by Barbara Ann Brenam, Bantam 1987.
2. Kundalini Yoga, by Swami Shivananda, (Shivananda Nagar), The Divine Life Society, 1971.
3. Maharishi's Gospel, The Teachings of Sri Ramana Maharishi, Sri Ramana Ashram, Tiruvannamali, India, 1999.
4. Sathyam Sivam Sundaram Series (Life Story of Bhagawan Sri Sathya Sai Baba), by Professor N. Kasturi, Sri Sathya Sai Books & Publications Trust, Prasanthi Nilayam, A.P. India.
5. The Bhagavad Gita.
6. The Bible.
7. The Gospel of Sri Ramakrishna vol. 1 & 11, by Mahendranath Gupta (M.), translated by Swami Nikhilananda, Sri Ramakrishna Math, India.
8. The Silva Mind Control Method by Jose Silva and Philip Miele, Pocket Books, New York, USA, 1977.
9. The Truth Is by Shri H.W.L. Poonja, Vidyasager Publications, San Anselmo, California, USA, 1995.
10. The Third Eye and Kundalini (An Experiential Account of Journey from Dust to Divinity) by B.S Goel, The Third Eye Foundation of India, Shri Siddheshwar Ashram, India, 1985.

CONTENTS

Part 3

Affirmations

Be Happy
with
Prayer, Meditation and Affirmation

Introduction

Prayer, Meditation and Affirmation are three Divine gifts to help us be in communion, union and glorification of God and the "Divine" within us. They are a manifestation of God's pure love and compassion for us and of God's glorification of us. They are Divine gifts to help us realise Love. By utilising these gifts we can be happy.

Communication with the Divine is never one-sided. What we desire from God is what God desires from us. What we request of God, is what God requests of us. When we ache and long for union, it is in actuality God's ache to unite with us. There is no division between God and us. We are one.

The idea that we are separated is mere illusion. But the beauty of this play of delusion is in the joy that comes when we achieve reunion. My Master, Bhagawan (God) Sri Sathya Sai Baba says:

I separated Myself from Myself in order that I may love Myself.
I am in you and you are in Me.

What Sai Baba is telling us in this statement is that we are a part of the Cosmic Power called God. He is declaring here that He knows that He is God. The only difference between Him and us is that He knows that He is God and we have not yet recognised that we are also God

When we know our truth and potential, our ability to unite with God is the real worth of all three gifts. They are gifts of Divine Love. Prayer, Meditation and Affirmation are actions and can be intrinsic in everything we do. For example, we can dance, sing or even eat with Divine intention, therefore making the action sacred. These gifts are the means to experience True Love in all forms.

Even though our compulsion to love is the ultimate and compelling drive within us we have forgotten that we are *Love* Itself. We have become lost through lifetimes of reaching for something other than our Divine Self. We ache and yearn to feel loved when we are that very Love Itself. We long for union with another when we are already Whole.

We will externally stop at nothing, try everything and anything, pay and sacrifice all we have, including sometimes our very souls for a tiny slither of what we think is love. Meanwhile, we celebrate selfish love such as lust, desire, infatuation, interdependence and co-dependency. All the while we turn our back on True Love which does not pick and choose, which celebrates Itself, is pure, is constant, has no judgement, and is all encompassing. True Love can never harm us. A heart filled with True Love cannot blame, criticise, or condemn, but allows everything, including Itself to be as it is. True Love can never be controlled by the ego. This is the real meaning of Self-Love.

We try to taste the nectar of this true Divine Love in our external relationships and partnerships while we ourselves are poisoned. What we reach out to is also poisoned and yet we think that this is what will save us. Each time we do this, we short-change our very selves. We turn our back on ourselves and betray ourselves.

And, deep in our present conditioning, we think that we have to sacrifice one for the other. We think that we cannot be Love and have Love. I have met so many people who have the idea that God, Spirituality or Divinity cannot be for them because they believe that they cannot renounce the world. When we conclude this, we turn or back on our spiritual potential because we think that we cannot be Love and enjoy the experience of Love in life.

Not only that, but when we hear stories of Liberated Beings who have a partner we may criticise these relationships because we think that they are sinful. Or, we think that these people cannot possibly be who or what they are commonly accepted to be. We think that somehow these people should not be involved in external life or in lovemaking and we condemn them from our own poisoned and limited perception. We do not realise that we as Divine Beings can celebrate Love in form.

There is a beautiful ancient Indian story contained in the *Yoga Vasishta*, (The Supreme Yoga) which exemplifies that Love and its Freedom can be experienced in living happily in married life.

Renounce the Ego, Not Life

King Sikhidhvaja and Queen Cudala have a great love for one another and rule their kingdom well. Unlike many marriages of the time, their marriage is a love match. They have everything they could possibly want. They have wealth, their kingdom and each other, but both realise that there can be something more, and they have a yearning to spiritually realise themselves. In this yearning, Cudala becomes enlightened and attains all spiritual and psychic powers. The King notices that she is different, that she radiates somehow, and that she grows younger looking. But even so, as Cudala tries to help her husband and enlighten him, he does not listen to her or believe her awareness and he laughs at her.

King Sikhidhvaja becomes more and more despondent as the time passes and he does not realise his longing for Spiritual Freedom. He decides that the only way he can find this is to renounce the world, enter the forest and live as an ascetic with all the austerities. He steals away in the night as the Queen sleeps and lives forgetting what he leaves behind and remains in prayer and meditation. Cudala is pained by her husband's actions. She had told him that this was not the answer for him and that this life of deprivation would not enlighten him, but with her psychic powers she sees that this has to be and that there is nothing she can do until a later time. So, Queen, Cudala remains in their kingdom to look after the affairs of state and their people.

For 18 years she dwells in the palace and King Sikhidhvaja in the forest. When Cudala realises that her husband's mind is ready for enlightenment, she flies through the sky with her powers to the forest to be with him. Even in her enlightened state, Cudala never lost the desire for her husband to find the spiritual freedom he so wished and she had remained all these years as his loving and faithful wife.

Cudala realises that even after all these years her husband may still not listen to her or believe her wisdom. With her psychic abilities she disguises herself as a young ascetic boy. On the appearance of the boy in the forest, the King is delighted to see him and worships him as a Celestial. In this way, Cudala is able to instruct her husband and prepare him for the elusive Liberation he has so much longed for.

As the ascetic boy, Cudala explains to her husband how just as the wealthy man searching for the Philosopher's Stone chose a piece of glass, he Sikhidhvaja, had abandoned the pursuit of pure, infinite consciousness for the pursuit of physical austerities which always have a beginning and an end. "One who abandons infinite joy for empty practices must surely be a fool," she explains to him.

Not only that, but in respect to renunciation she tells him, "Wealth, wife, palace, kingdom, the earth and the royal umbrella and your relatives are not yours, O king. Renouncing them does not constitute total renunciation! There is something else which seems to be yours and which you have not renounced, and that is the best part of renunciation. Renounce that totally and without any residue and attain freedom from sorrow." Cudala continued with many instances of similar reasoning until eventually, the King's mind was ready to hear, "Uproot the tree whose seed is I with all its branches, fruits and leaves and rest in the space of the heart."

With the awareness of what the words meant, Sikhidhvaja awakened to his Divinity. He realised that he was not the "doer" of his actions. His renunciation of wife, wealth and kingdom that he thought would free his mind could only damage his ignorance, but never kill it.

Cudala, in the guise of the ascetic boy, continued to teach Sikhidhvaja until he was fully grounded in the Truth, and when the time was ripe she revealed her real identity to him. He was overjoyed with her and realised her worth as his wife as well as his teacher. His gratitude and love for her continued for as long as they were together on this earth plane.

King Sikhidhvaja and Queen Cudala triumphantly returned to their kingdom mounted on a stately elephant, At her husband's request, they were accompanied with an entire army created by Cudala's thought form. When they reached the outskirts of their city their citizens gave them a rousing welcome. It is said that they ruled their kingdom for a period of 10,000 years after which the King attained Nirvana (Final Liberation, like a lamp that burns without oil) from which there is no rebirth.

Finally, Vasistha's commentary to Rama about the moral of this story was... "O Rama, engage yourself in spontaneous and natural activity, without grief. Arise. Enjoy the pleasures of the world and also final Liberation."

This profound and enlightening story clearly reveals to us that Liberation and the means towards it is not to do with renunciation and austerities of the world, but about the renunciation of our ego sense of self. It is our awareness of and renunciation of the mind, its play of thoughts and its intrinsic attachment and desires for the world that is the key to Liberation. In this way, we can be in the world but not of it.

For some spiritual aspirants, the path of renunciation is perfect. But if you do not feel that it is right for you, there is no need to feel guilty or to feel that your spiritual path is a lesser one or hopeless. Sai Baba tells us to place our *"Minds in the forest and our hands in society."*

At this critical time, when the forces of good and evil seem to be engaged in an all-out war, it is imperative that as many of us as possible, who are on a spiritual path, do not renounce the world but stay in it. In this way we can be present to help ease the difficulties that are on this planet in whichever way we can. For example, we can use the spiritual advances we gain to help care for one another rather than retreat from the world and its problems. People are needed to help war victims, to help the starving masses, to find ways to bring water where there is drought, and most importantly to help our Earth that is severely wounded with toxins and pollution. On the simplest level, as spiritual aspirants we have a duty to be at least kind and considerate to our families, friends and neighbours. This is love and prayer in action.

I do not remember that God ever said to us that as Beings of Love we could not enjoy life. How is it that we were programmed to feel that if we know ourselves as Divine Love that we cannot enjoy its expression in our lives and relationships ? The truth is that we can. The truth is that in knowing ourselves as complete Love we are truly capable of expressing external love and living life in its fullness without grief.

Our primary and real Love is the love of God, the love of God within us. The love of "Love" Itself. Yet, because of our desires, our lack of realisation of them and our fears, some have come to hate God. Many people find it difficult now to even connect with the very idea of God, let alone love God. Many people, when they think of God, experience anger, fear, helplessness, abandonment or feelings of unworthiness.

If our primary love is the love of "God", this of course colours every other form of love relationship we have. How we relate to God is how we relate to everyone and everything else. On the other hand, if we have a split in this fundamental love, we have pain, not only in all our relationships with others, but also with our selves on all levels. This division and pain does not end with death. For example, if we do not heal this split in this lifetime, we will enter the subtle worlds carrying it and be reborn with it. Our next birth will mirror the extent of the split we have as we die.

Even if there is the acknowledgement of the need to heal this split with God, to allocate some time to be with God, it is kept apart from "real life", what we think has priority or what is really important. God time is not priority time! The time for God, for connecting to one's Divinity, to one's True Love is spent as time apart. This in itself leads to a deeper, further split within us. This is how Prayer, Meditation and Affirmation as they are commonly practised split us even more.

There are night-time prayers or a half-hour meditation in the morning or in the evening. There is an hour Sunday service at Church or Sunday school. How can we have fallen into serving ourselves so poorly? How can we bear this split, this starvation from our true nourishment? In so much fasting, mankind is now spiritually starved and emaciated whilst being externally fat and full.

We have become satiated with food, indulgences, comforts, desires and external longings. We are loaded with everything that burdens us, which is short-lived and which we can only have on loan and never permanently. Not only that, we borrow from the reservoir of our True Selves. We use up that God-given energy, create a debt and put ourselves in slavery.

It is as if we borrow from a bank to own a second rate house, pay high interest payments for the rest of our days, and then die exhausted and unfulfilled, never having owned the property. In the meantime of our lives, we have tired ourselves out having to work long hard hours to make the money for the payments, unable to enjoy God, our families, life itself in its Truth. In reality, we never got the wealth we could have had. We never got the abode that was always waiting for us. All we needed to do was to claim it.

We immerse ourselves in a river of grief and at every moment turn away from our birthright. We are creatures of habit and we have got into this habit of forgetting our true inheritance.

We have become so split, so removed from our Garden of Eden that we have even come to hate God. I cannot imagine that God ever cast us out of Eden. Our desires, our seeking outward towards the temporary, the illusory, the unreal, led us into thinking that we left Paradise. Actually, we are still there. We have merely turned away from the true beauty and have become charmed by the illusion.

As well as this, there is also little known joy in the communication, union or honouring of the Divine in our lives. When we pray, it is usually because of pain, trauma, and desperation. Implicit is expectation. We do not commune to feel joy or to celebrate joy, but because we want something we do not have, or because we do not want to have something. When we meditate we try to achieve and to fill our egos with a sense of self worth in the doing. It becomes a "doing" rather than a "being" and we become frustrated, bored and feel inadequate. We have forgotten how to connect and what the connection was all about in the first place.

By Praying, Meditating and Affirming with awareness, we can heal this division and delusion and become at one with Love. We can be happy.

Part 1
Prayer

Prayer

In the Beginning

1

What is prayer? Whom or what are we really praying to? What is the purpose of prayer? What is the point of prayer? Why do we pray? These are questions that many people have come to ask. Actually, these questions should be asked again and again until we feel sure and secure in knowing what prayer is about.

Do you remember as a child having to, as I was instructed to, learn to pray by heart? In reality, the heart for me had little to do with this learning. Rather, what was expected of me, was to learn the words like a parrot until they were imbedded in my mind, word for word. Perhaps this was your experience and just as I did, you recited them daily. The following is a common experience of many people's childhood with prayer:

A child learns a prayer. Usually the first prayer we learn to say parrot fashion is the Lord's Prayer. After some time, perhaps even from the very beginning, the words of the prayer mean very little to the child. But still the child is expected to say the prayer. After some more time, the child does not want to say the prayer anymore because from meaning only a little to the child, the prayer now means absolutely nothing. The child even feels resentful about having to say the prayer at all.

The Lord's Prayer is a beautiful prayer. But a five or six year-old child cannot find much meaning in it. The words and the way they are used are not the natural way a child talks. It is true that there can be something comforting in reciting what feels like sacred words. And when these words have been used for centuries in a sacred manner they hold a power. But where is the "gripping" connection in the words of such a sophisticated prayer for a child? How can a child connect with prayer in a way that will help to allow the child to feel the words and to experience the words as Divine and as God?

Unfortunately, we often get stuck in the way we are conditioned and programmed as children and this also applies to the way we relate and pray to God. Even if we think that this is not pertinent to us, we are still subtly affected. How can we not be? Consider for a moment about how you were first introduced to the concept of God and prayer. This happening was a definite initial imprinting. This imprinting will most probably have influenced you and will be continuing to influence you in your relationship to God and prayer. Unless understood and exorcised it will also influence your future *potential* relationship with God and prayer.

Even if you did not have any personal religious teaching, there will be a subtle effect on you from the influence of the society you were brought up in and its connection to God and prayer. The basic truth is that we likewise physically inherit any split our teachers had when they first introduced us to these concepts. Can you remember whether you felt your divinity teacher, priest, minister, parent or society to be at one with God? Did they manifest love? Were they happy? Did they celebrate prayer? Were they respectful and did they have gratitude? Did they honour and cherish you? If not, there is little likelihood that you can easily connect with these qualities either. In the same way, it has most probably been an ongoing struggle for you. And also you will have a tendency to feel the same kind of relationship to God and prayer as they did or do.

Many children of course do feel an immense and naturally innate connection to the Divine, to God. They feel "at home" with any talk of God or even prayer. Often, the younger a child the more ease the child has with the idea of God and prayer. External ideas and concepts of others have not yet tarnished their connection. The outside and physical world and its enticements have not yet taken a strong hold of the child's admissible mind and the innate Divinity can be nurtured and given a strong protective shield. If children can be God-nurtured at this early time in his/her life, they will have the spiritual basis to help them grow with God.

There is an ancient Hindu story of the Homa bird:

The Homa Bird

The Homa bird lives very high in the sky and there the mother bird lays her egg. She lives so high that the egg falls for many, many days.

While it is falling the egg is hatched. The chick also continues to fall for many days. In the meantime, because of the time this takes, the chick develops eyes. Coming near the Earth, it becomes aware of the world and realises that it will meet its death as it crashes to the ground. The chick gives a shrill cry and shoots up towards its mother. For the chick, the Earth means death and it is so frightened it seeks its mother, residing high up in the sky. The young bird goes straight to her. It does not even try to look anywhere else.

The moral of this story is that we need to realise the danger of coming in contact with the world. People born with a strong connection to God know this from their very childhood and are afraid of the world, of falling into it and crashing. All of us to various degrees have a sense of the danger awaiting us. All of us have the inherent ability to shoot to God just as the chick so easily found its mother. Children who are encouraged to continue their innate connection with God, through their mother or father or lives, have a head start in the flight back to Divinity.

The Tibetan Buddhists also talk of the blessing of receiving a good human rebirth and what this really means. One of the important criteria of a good human birth is to be born where one will be introduced at an early age to a religious educational training in some form, to be born into a family that is connected with some form of religion. To the Tibetan Buddhists it does not matter whether that education is Buddhist, Hindu, Christian, Muslim—whatever. What matters to them is that spiritual help is available at the most critical time of a child's connection to its own Divinity.

We, as children, are like the little Homa chick or like little baby God trees, full of the potential to become the Divine Tree of Life Itself. But, until that expression of our Divinity has fully taken root, we need to be protected and nourished.

Western children who receive spiritual guidance are often conditioned to believe in God as a benevolent father figure seated on a throne in heaven or as a kindly Jesus with many children surrounding Him in happiness. Children are taught to pray to Him to take care of them. This can be very comforting for a child. But is it enough?

Eastern children who receive spiritual teaching have a galaxy of Gods and Goddesses to choose from as an image of Divinity in form. These expressions of Divinity are extremely colourful and enchanting but their very numbers might be confusing. Yet, both these Eastern and Western children who have been introduced to the concept of God are the fortunate ones. They are like the Homa chick, already flying in the sky towards their true mother and father. But there is a multitude of other children who are crashing to the ground.

There are millions of children living on Earth now, who receive no inspiration, teaching of God, no instruction of prayer and do not even know what prayer is. They are growing up worshipping the material world, with an emphasis fully on the vast array of toys and games on offer in department stores, on TV, on radio, everywhere. Their Gods are beings like Santa Claus and the latest "in" TV series heroes. At a very early age they even begin shopping on the Web. There is actually no Divinity out there for them. As they grow into adults their idols become cricket players, footballers, singers, movie stars and they devote themselves to power dressing, power socialising and worshipping power tycoons. As a result, the nearest concept to prayer is the demand "I want".

Paradoxically, at the very same time, the majority of the world's children still do not have enough to eat and are experiencing intense poverty and physical deprivation. Consequently, these children are also currently deprived of the concept of God. Their families are starving and just finding food and water consumes their entire energy. There is no time for them to receive or even have access to spiritual teachers and education.

The aforementioned millions of human beings who have worldly abundance but who are lost to their own Divinity have little compassion and watch apathetically the latter billions who have nothing. It is the apathetic who have sold their souls to the Devil of Temporary Pleasure and Satisfaction.

Of course, none of the above may apply to you but it is a good beginning to ponder a little on how your early experiences may be affecting you and how your children are being affected by their experience. In realising the influences, you will be able to break the last bonds of any conditioning squeezing out the Divine life in you. Prayer cuts through the traps of illusion outlined above and it opens your heart to your own Divinity. Let us begin now. We have no choice.

Prayer and God

2

Firstly, let us ask the question "What is prayer?" Prayer is not just talking to God. If so, the word "prayer" would be substituted by the word "talk.' The word and its meaning are important. The word prayer tells us that what is involved here is more than just saying some words. It is more than mere talk. It is asking something else from us. What could that be? What can be asked of us here? It is important to consider these questions deeply for here is the initial possible potential of our oneness with God or our split with God.

Words and talking are an intrinsic part of our lives but not prayer. Prayer has been split from our "normal daily life". Talking with some people is almost constant. Prayer has been isolated to special times and places and for special reasons and requests. This is a further reflection of our split with God.

So how can we pray to God? Prayer is talking with God. It is communicating our selves through words to God. But with the respectful awareness that we, as Divine Beings, are talking and communicating with God Who is Divine. It is that simple and yet that holy. It is that common and yet that sacred. If we wish to celebrate this communication ritualistically we can. If at any moment in our day we feel the need to have a conversation and talk as one would with a friend, we can. If we feel that we wish to talk something over we do. How can we ever be lonely with such a Divine friend and companion, with such a relationship? Yet sometimes we do feel alone and bereft when we forget to pray.

Who are we praying to? If we ask anyone that question they would most likely answer, "to God." But then, Who is God? Is God the benevolent father figure seated on a throne in heaven, or Jesus smiling at us? Is God Ganesha, that beautifully round Hindu being with the elephant head, who when we pray to him, removes obstacles for us? From the array of images of Gods and different religions, it looks like God comes in many forms. We really do not need to argue about which one is the right one. All are correct. None have got it wrong. What is important in this array is that many people need

God to have a form personal to them and this helps them to relate to God. What has happened is that larger groups of like-minded people with the same kind of preference have made a religion out of that liking or form and this has helped them to remember God.

There are also many people who feel more comfortable in relating to God as formless. For example, God can be thought of as Cosmic Consciousness. Like the whole universe, we are temporary forms of the Cosmic Power called God. Like us, any forms of God are merely temporary and are an appearance of the Power or Source called God.

We can identify with any of these groups and feel personally connected to its imagery of God. But we do not necessarily need other people's ideas of God's form or formlessness. We can create a personal image in our mind about what God looks like to us. This image does not need to be static. It can change as we change.

Actually, the object of your devotion is not as important as the devotion itself. Your devotion itself is the Divinity, is God, and when it is firmly rooted in you, no one can ever take it away from you. It is like the following story:

The God Box

Imagine that you are a young child being told by someone whom you firmly trust that God is contained in a certain little box. You are given the box to keep and to pray to. Because you totally believe that God is in the box and you wish to be close to God, you take the box containing God everywhere with you. Other people find out what you are doing and what you believe in, but you do not care when they make fun of you or taunt you. Their words cannot shatter your faith. You know that God is in the box no matter what they say. Over the years, you and God become very close. You pray and perform sacred rituals to your little box. You honour your box daily. You polish it and protect it and keep it clean.

You talk to your box often and you are assured that you are always heard. God does not let you down. Whenever you need any help, you ask God in the box to help you and miraculous things happen to help you. You have stories of how many times this has happened for you and the proof of how good God is.

Time passes and you become an old lady or gentleman and you are at one with your box. You are so happy that God has come to you like this. The gift of the box and the presence of God throughout your life have been a wonder and a treasure for you. This connection to God through your little box has made your life feel full and worth while. You are even happy to die because you know now that you and God are so close you will never be parted.

Mynavati

What is important here? Is it the box or the faith and devotion towards the box? It does not matter, if for you, God is a box. God is everywhere and in everything. What matters is your consistency of devotion and your appreciation of the gift of God.

God is Divinity. In talking with God, in praying to God, we are communicating with Divinity, as Divinity, to Divinity. In this way of being we can include God in everything we do, and feel full and whole. When we walk, work, eat, love, play and even sleep, we can include God and feel full, whole and be happy. When we forget to talk to God in prayer and we forget to include God in our lives we are empty, lost and potentially devastated. Everything we have is subject to change. At times life will be good to us and at other times it will not be so good. Regardless of what life gives you or does not, you can have prayer and communion with God and the permanent happiness that this gives you. No one can take this away from you.

If you treasure your box, it will become Divine and invincible and no one will be able to steal it away from you or even damage it. It will always be yours and yours alone. In this way God loves each of us so uniquely and perfectly.

Why Pray ?

3

Why do we need to pray? If we are told that we are Divine, then why do we need to bother? We may be Divine, but we do not behave as, believe in, know, or actualise, Divinity. That is why we need to pray. We are helpless, we are suffering and we have no other choice. Actually, when we realise that from the vantage of our ego self and its mind games and confusion, prejudices and projections, we can never have the answers, we will never stop praying. We will not be able to stop, for we will realise just how lost we are. We pray because we need God more than anything or anyone else in the world. We pray because we know that the small "I" can never be enough.

Then, of course, there is the idea of gratitude. When was the last time that you prayed out of absolute gratitude and not because you wanted anything from God? We usually pray demanding something or someone. We are only aware of what we do not have and which we want, and we demand God to give it to us. We are like little children who have our eyes on a small piece of cake that has been given to our brother or sister. All we are thinking about is that we want the same piece that has been given to them. We cannot take our eyes off it. That piece of cake becomes the centre of our universe and it is all we can focus on. We are paining because they are getting it and we are not. We watch them as they take every small piece into their mouth and swallow it. We become obsessed and we become angry and feel mad because they have it, have enjoyed it and we did not. This is an example of desire, jealousy and envy, and this is how our emotions and feelings trap us.

In fact, because of our feelings, we have completely forgotten that it is our birthday and we can have as much cake as we wish. It is *always* our birthday and our very own delicious and huge birthday cake complete with candles is right under our noses. But all the time, our eyes are centred on this tiny slither of cake that someone else has got, and so we cannot see our own special cake. We cannot smell it, we cannot taste it and we cannot begin to appreciate and enjoy the love and attention that has been poured into it for us. We ruin our whole birthday party because we only want what we think was better and which went to someone else instead. This is how many of us live our lives.

God, in complete and utter Love, has given us a huge *life* birthday party complete with cake, candles, games, celebration, friends, relatives and TIME. God is pouring that love on us in every moment, just as it was poured into the cake. But are we grateful? As the TIME passes, do we say thank you to God? Do we notice what we have? Or, do we just take it all for granted and instead continually demand something else from God– do we ask for something that we know someone else has had and which we want instead? We constantly whine for something we think God has never given us. But what about what God has given us? Instead of demanding for anything else, we need to say, "Thank you, God."

We need to feel grateful and thank God again and again and again until we really understand how much love is being given to us. We need to fully appreciate what we have before we consider asking God for anything else.

Bearing this in mind, I mentally asked God about what I can pray for and the immediate internal response I got back was, "Anything."

"Anything?" I asked. God again answered, "Yes, anything, but never come to me as a beggar or a bargainer." Now, this is quite a statement. I wondered, does this mean that I should ask God as an equal?

I realise that God does not want me to plead or to be ingratiating. God wants me to know that I am to honour also that I am Divine. So, I can ask God for anything, on equal terms. But I understand that if I have any respect for God, I need to ask with humility, with the knowledge that God knows better than I do. I do so because my awareness is tainted through the colouring of egoistic eyes. I therefore ask:

Dear God, Let it be Thy will and not my will.
For You alone know best what is good for me in all ways and for all concerned.

If I ask with humility and in awareness of my Divinity as God's beloved child, I can ask for anything and I am never a beggar or a bargainer. A bargainer says to God, "If you do this for me, I will do this for you." But God is not interested in anything you can offer. God is not interested in anything we have to offer because whatever we have and hold belongs to God in the first place, and God has loaned it out to us. How can we bargain with something we do not even own? We have absolutely no collateral with God. Even our very egos belong to God, and we can only give them back to God when God allows us to surrender them. But, what we can give God is our Love and Devotion.

If I ask God anything with an awareness of my Divinity and an acceptance that God knows best what is for me, I have no other option but to hand my request over and surrender it to God. This is actually a relief and gives me something else to be grateful to God about. It gives me another reason to love God.

If we have no gratitude, humility, or respect we are on the way to following Lucifer who was so beautiful, so clever and the most light-filled of God's Angels. In fact, he was God's very own favourite. But for Lucifer this was not enough. He lost his humility and he thought he did not need God any more. After his fall and after he was cast out of heaven, perhaps Lucifer thought that he had lost God's Love forever. What would have happened if he had prayed to God? It looks like he didn't, and as a result he has taken the role of trying to persuade everyone to join him in his torture. Filled with darkness, he became known as Satan and he has lived within us ever since. He waits for us to merge with him and to forget God.

We repeat this satanic action every day in our lives when we feel unhappy and we want to make others suffer too. We repeat this action when we let go of God and allow or egos to take control of us. We continue in this ignorant way until we realise that regardless of what we do or have done, God never stops loving us and is enduringly there for us. God will never go away and leave us. It is we who turn away from God and think that there is something better to have and to hold.

When we fully realise that there is darkness within us too, as well as light, we will pray unceasingly. We can pray knowing that God knows best. We can pray for anything that means something to us. It need not be something so called *spiritual.* It can be something *worldly*. Everything is God. What matters in the desire and asking of anything is our motivation. Perhaps we would like a new car, or a husband, or a wife, or we are lonely or sad and we do not want to feel like that anymore. Maybe we also want to pray for someone else. We have all kinds of wishes and desires. There is nothing wrong in praying for worldly things rather than spiritual gifts. In this relative word, we are human after all, as well as Divine and God understands that. Divinity does not judge. It is only the ego that judges.

Then there is the question of "Can we demand?" When I teach workshops this question is asked a number of times. I reason, of course we can demand an answer from God. Can a child not demand love from its mother or father? Can a child not demand to know if its mother and father are listening to its questions and cries? You are a child of God. You are God's very own. You can demand to know, "When, why not, and how long?"

What is silly for us is to demand the *outcome* when we know God knows best. This is not only silly but shows a lack of trust, of faith and it suggests that we think we know best...better than God. A child can demand food from the mother and father, can even demand to know what time it will get this food. The child can say what dish it likes best and its preferences, but the child has to trust the mother and father about the nutrition of the food, about the diet and whether it is the right one or not.

Left to their own choices, many three-year-olds might pick a diet of chocolate and fizzy juice. A child's mother and father will choose a different, much more nutritious diet altogether. We are generally not even as bright or as intelligent as three- year-olds in our knowing of what is good for us. God alone knows our past, present and future. This is why it is silly of us to ask God for the outcome. We can tell God our preferences and we can ask God to help us with them, but we should get out of the habit of dictating to God as though we know better.

Many of us, when we want something, act like three-year-olds, and if we do not get that thing we want or even at the time we want it, we get very upset and we go into a tantrum. God hears these demands and tantrums everyday, all day. Perhaps it's time we gave God a break and pleasantly surprised God!

Just for one day, let's talk to God, Divinity to Divinity, in respect and humility, pouring out to God our hearts and what is within our souls, and then hand it all over. Let us allow God to take care of our requests and us. Let us lean on God and relax and just enjoy our birthday party.

In every moment that we can remember, in every day, let us thank God for what has actually been given to us and for what is being given to us always.

Prayer and Heart

4

Have you ever had a conversation with someone who is speaking to you and their voice is droning on and on in a seemingly hollow and empty way? It is as if they are talking just for the sake of talking but there is nobody there? You definitely do not feel as though they are talking to you. You are just "something", a kind of trapped energy which is there, and there is some pretence going on that you are even the recipient of the words. And the words arouse absolutely no feeling in, and have no meaning to, the speaker, let alone any connection to you. In fact, you as the listener want to go to sleep and, as the words drone on, you do.

I remember experiencing this as a therapist when a client would come and talk just for the sake of talking. They just wanted to use up their "therapeutic hour." Or, they would not be speaking authentically, or with any feeling. They were totally out of touch with what was really going on. Once or twice as I experienced this, I fell asleep, and I awoke as my head jerked violently backward. I remember feeling embarrassed. It must have been the most comical sight to behold. But the person who was talking to me was so far away from being present that they did not even notice what had happened. Another time, as I felt myself drift into a possible snore, I just had to say truthfully to the person, 'You are boring me.' Actually, the session went very well after my comment. It shook my client into awareness and a connection to what they were saying and they experienced quite an insight that was just not possible before.

Have you ever become irritated when a checkout clerk will falsely smile at you and vacantly say something like, "How are you today, Madam?" Then after you pay your bill and are leaving that person shouts to you, "Thank you. Have a good day. Come again." People are actually trained to do this and we are indoctrinated in society now to accept this polite but false way of being. I have looked up or turned around and sometimes these people are not even looking at me. It's just words. And it is such a waste of energy when there is no feeling or heart to our words.

The same condition can exist with prayer when we just regurgitate the sacred words or when we pray merely for the sake of praying. Why bother to do that? Why go to all that trouble and use that energy just to put God to sleep or to bore God. Why should God listen to hollow or polite words? God wants our hearts. God does not want our empty words. God wants our passion and our intensity. God is not interested in our politeness.

And, I am sure, God does not want us to hurry up our conversation so that we can do something more important like catch the bus, or meet one of our friends with whom we are going to have an incredibly in-depth conversation instead. Perhaps we are even going to talk about God. But what about *how* we are talking *with* God? Why be so insulting? On some level, we really are insulting, or we are buying into the false notion that prayer and God are not of any great value to us, or we would just not do that!

What God wants is not empty words but communication from you. God wants communion with you in that communication. God wants the language of the heart. God wants your words with the intense feeling of this communication.

How can a prayer ever be of value without love? How can a heart be real without love? How can a mantra say or do anything without the fuel of commitment and passion?

Without feeling, without this language of the heart, we are not human beings. We are flesh, blood and bone and we breathe, but we are not alive. We are like Zombies, like the walking dead. One just needs to walk down a city High Street and one will see many of these Zombies. We do not have to go to the cinema to see a horror movie to observe a Zombie. All we need to do is get out of touch with our feelings, disconnect from our heart and the light goes out of us, and we become blackened by darkness. What can God offer us then? What is the point of God listening to a Zombie, and does a Zombie care about what anyone has to say, let alone God?

From the age of around three years old, I had a recurring dream/nightmare:

The Zombie Dream

I am wearing a blue gingham dress and beautiful red shoes. My hair is tied in ribbons and I am so happy because I know I am with God. I am in God's garden and it is O, so beautiful. The sky is bluer than any blue sky I can remember, and the grass is greener than any grass I have ever seen. And I am so happy. I can hear bells ringing in the background, like the peal of church bells, and I can hear children laughing and giggling, as if at play. I am so happy to hear this sound but I have no need to join the other children because I am content within myself.

Then, I am aware of many, many people, walking towards me, as though they are dead. Their expression is of a deep, deep depression. Yet, like Zombies, they also seem alive and they are walking in God's garden. But they are unaware of where they are and they do not even notice me. I run up in front of them and I try to make them see me. I am telling them that they are in this beautiful garden, God's garden, but they neither see nor hear me. They just walk on past. I am haunted and upset by the lack of awareness and, as a result, my own happiness is wiped out.

This recurrent nightmare and its evocative imagery has stayed with me my entire life. Its effect has been to push me more to God and for that I am grateful. The memory of the scenes and the look of the adults have increasingly taken my spiritual naivete away over the years.

From birth I was a restless child and could not sleep well at night. During these nightmare episodes, I remember sitting up in my bed and praying fervently to God to take me "home" before I became like these people. In my small and simple child mind I assumed that if I grew up I would be like this too.

Then, suddenly when I was nine years old, I got the choice of dying or of growing up:

A True Story

It was the first time I went to the swimming baths with a small group of children and I was so excited I forgot to take off even my socks and wristwatch. I was the first one changed into my swimsuit and the first one at the poolside. I remember looking into the water and not knowing how deep it was. I did not know if it was the deep end or the shallow end of the pool. I had never been in a pool before and I knew nothing about swimming. As I looked into the water I heard a thought come into my mind which said, "Just jump. If it is the shallow end you will be all right, and if it is the deep end you will automatically be able to swim, or you will drown and go home."

So, I jumped and it was the deep end. I sank to the bottom and then unexpectedly bobbed up, took a breath of air and went back down again. This happened a few more times. The next thing I knew I was on the surface of the water taking a deep breath, and I knew I would not be able to get back up the next time. I saw a lifeguard at some point during this experience, but he did not notice me.

I sank back to the bottom of the pool and everything around me seemed to be dissolving and growing lighter, including myself. At this point, I saw two scenes open up on either side of me. Strangely, I do not know if my eyes were open or shut, or if I was conscious or unconscious. In retrospect, I think I was leaving my body.

The scene on my left showed me my mother and father opening the door to a policeman who went on to explain to them that I, their only child, had drowned in the pool. I was shocked by my mother's and my father's grief. I had never realised, before seeing this vision, what it would mean to them if I really did go home to God.

Simultaneously, I viewed the scene on my right. Like the scene on my left, it was only about three feet away from me. In this view, I saw myself running up to the door of my house and being greeted happily by my mother and father.

At that point, the predicament of my parents touched my heart and I felt it open towards them in a way that I did not understand. Now I know my feeling was of intense compassion for them because I saw and was aware how much they loved and needed me.

When this feeling of compassion flooded my heart, I awoke at the poolside being resuscitated by some blurry people at my side. They were pressing my abdomen and water was coming out of my mouth. The first thing I noticed was that I was wearing my wristwatch and I had my white ankle socks on.

I have no idea how long the entire "drowning" experience took. I only know that this was one of the first spiritual experiences I had.

Of course, God did not take me to where I thought was home. I am glad that God did not let me opt out then or beforehand and gave me the grace to stay in my body this far. One of the great realisations about prayer that has come to me from this experience is that our hearts are pure and they know the truth. My heart, on seeing the views of my possible fates, became filled with compassion and it was my immediate connection to Divinity.

My heart took the decision for me to remain on Earth, so that I am able to know and enjoy God's garden here. In the end, our hearts and God are one. This is why Eastern Religion tells us that our actual hearts are the seats of the Divine. I found, through this happening, that prayer can be transmitted or received at any moment, for our hearts are always connected to the Divine. What's more, I realised that our hearts pray for us constantly!

Therefore, the original, frightening Zombie dream turned out to be a very powerful spiritual teaching, even though I was a child. Its effect pushed me into fervently praying to God. I prayed with my whole heart. I talked to God all night. I knew I had to. If I did not, and if I did not get God to listen to me and "beam me up" I was facing that terror of becoming like these Zombie people.

What I know now is that we are all in God's garden and we can all be happy. We can all be content in our love for God no matter where we are. Heaven and God's garden is not somewhere else. It is here and now. Our love and communication, communion with God, is anytime we want to talk with God.

The only hindrance to our knowing this is our lack of heart, lack of connection, lack of awareness, lack of gratitude. When we are like this we are Zombies. When we connect with our heart and its language, we are instantly in communication and prayer with God.

Prayer by Letter

5

The bird with you, the wings with Me;
The foot with you, the way with Me;
The eye with you, the form with Me;
The thing with you, the dream with Me;
The world with you, the heaven with Me –
So are we free, so are we bound;
So we begin and so we end;
You in Me and I in you.

Sri Sathya Sai Baba

During these early experiences with God and prayer I remember that as soon as I could read and write I would also write little letters to God. Of course, they were all in the same theme of wanting God to, "Please take me home." I would write these letters and wait for an answer. A child's mind focuses on the one and only possible answer for them. Children have a pretty fixed black and white view of the world. And so I waited for God to suddenly lift me up to heaven. I believed that this would happen.

My mind was not open to the idea that God could answer us in many ways, and so I was not open to other options than the one I was mentally fixated on. But still, I liked the idea of writing to God, even when I did not get the reply I wanted; and I did not stop doing this until a certain point in my life when I turned my back on God for some years. When that happened, I was not interested in the very idea of God, let alone in writing letters.

Later, when I renewed my connection with God, realising then that although I had abandoned God, God had actually never abandoned me. God had held and cared for me throughout this period waiting for me to come out of my mood. God is very patient and even if it had taken many lifetimes for me to change my disposition, God would still be waiting. At this point, I had begun working with people as a psychotherapist and healer and, when appropriate, I would share my experiences of connecting to God with my clients. The idea of writing a letter to God also helped them very much.

I saw then, that in connecting with Divinity and in praying through writing, people who were feeling blocked or hopeless were often able to become unstuck, move through and be lifted from the narrow view of the mind and its fixed idea of how things should be. In praying in this very focussed way, they found that some opening could happen, some insight, intuition, some feeling of response or answer would come for them.

We can never solve our problems with the mind. It is the mind that has composed the problem. It is the mind and its ensemble of thoughts that have given you the pain and the suffering, so of course it can never come up with the solution. Whatever solution the mind comes up with will only immerse you further in a dilemma.

I observed that what is helpful when people pray to God with writing, is that they have a record of what they wrote. They have something concrete that they can look at again and be able to view in a different way. Their minds are clearly able to read what is written and know the pickle it is in, and in that awareness there comes humility. With humility, we can formally, respectfully and gratefully hand the whole thing over to God. To whom else can we do this? Who else is really available to us with the necessary Divine Wisdom? Who else really cares *always*?

There are some very powerful reasons which make the writing of words as a prayer so helpful in Divine Connection. Firstly, it requires some effort from us to write something in the form of a letter, and this is good if we want to communicate with God. This is because it requires some commitment from us, and I am sure that when we give some effort and commitment in our communication with Divinity, this pleases God. So, in endeavouring to write, we cannot just glibly say empty words without the thought of any commitment.

We have "to write" the words. We have to make the time to write the words and obtain the necessary materials. We have to find the pen, the paper and even some surface to write on. We try not to be disturbed. This all requires effort. One cannot "hurry" a letter quite in the same way one can hurry up a "Hello", whilst running off somewhere. When we get this far in writing a letter to God, we can at least know that we think God and us are worth the effort. This is a big step in the right direction towards owning our Divinity.

Secondly, in writing a letter, rather than in speaking, one can focus the mind more easily. If you become readily distracted while praying with words, or find it difficult to connect with your feelings at that time, you may find it easier to have more of a connection in writing a letter to God. This centring may also help you to access the authenticity of your feelings. Also, when we write and we become relaxed with the process, we can allow our expression to flow, and we sometimes begin to write something we never even thought of. We can surprise ourselves with what we write down. I have often found in these instances that when people just allow the words to flow, they are amazed at what they have written. When we access our feelings in this way and allow ourselves to open up to God we can more and more allow our hearts to pour out to God. This can become a beautiful process and with an unexpected turn of events.

Some people have told me how they have used their left hand to write rather than their right hand (that is, when they are right handed) and that this has helped them further to bypass the ego mind and connect more with the heart. Some people choose a particular time of the day and make this a special period, which also helps them to immediately connect and be present to what they are doing. Some friends paint the most beautiful pictures and colour drawings and honour God in this way. They may use words with their art, or they may not.

After writing the letter, some people like to place the prayer letter under their pillows. Often when this is done, Divine love and help will come through the night in the form of a dream, or as a feeling, an insight on awakening. There are myriad ways to pray by letter. Others carry the letter around with them and consequently feel that God is with them throughout the day.

In a time of crisis, for example, when someone contacts me to tell me that they are in pain or there has been an accident or some situation that is critical, I will often write a small letter to God and place it under a lighted candle. This little ritual of prayer has sometimes worked seeming miracles. I place the letter under the candle and then light it with the intention:

Dear God, Let there be Light in this situation.
Let it be Thy Will and not my will.

I have a friend who had a cat for many years. One day she contacted me in terrible distress. Her cat was old by that time, very old even by cat standards, and now seemed to be dying. The cat would not drink or eat anything and was just lying in a corner. My friend had at that time been experiencing the most profound loss in her life. The year had been filled with death and disaster. She could not face the thought of also losing her beloved cat. I told her that I would light a candle for the little cat that evening. I did so, as in the way described above, and I received a phone call the following day from my friend. She told me that at some point in the evening, (We later ascertained that it was at around the time I lit the candle.) the cat who had been lying listless and without any energy suddenly jumped up, shook itself as cats do, and decided to have a drink.

The cat happily lived for another couple of years and then died peacefully. This is an example of the power of prayer. Only God in compassion could heal the cat and help my friend. Only God could decide that to allow the cat to live for another two years was the most compassionate and appropriate action for both of them. I am sure also that the cat, in its deep love and gratitude for my friend, was a willing and happy recipient of God's decree. I am convinced that the cat's own Divinity wished to help its beloved carer, my friend, as well as be an instrument of God.

God alone knows what is best for us and when. As I wrote earlier, I usually include in my letters and prayers to God, the phrase,

Let it be Thy will and not my will.

As well as that phrase, I also try to remember to write or say,

For the good of all concerned.

We, with our identification to ego-mind cannot understand the action that is appropriate for the good of all concerned. This is the exclusive wisdom of God.

Not long after I met my Guru, Sai Baba, He beautifully acknowledged my love of communicating to God in prayer by letter, and He allowed me to pour out to Him all that I felt I needed to and which was in my heart up to that time.

For a period of around four weeks, Sai Baba was giving two Darshans (views of God in form) a day at Kodaikanal, a hill station in India. Each day, twice a day, I wrote letters to Him as God. He came to me and took the letters from me. Sometimes, if He did not take the letters in the morning, He would take them in the afternoon. In this way, I engaged in an intense communication with Him. I found that as I wrote daily in this way to my Guru, that more and more words and feelings came. I just handed over to Him all that was in my heart, all that had been troubling me and which was holding me back from my opening my heart more. This went on for the weeks that I was there. Eventually, I felt there was nothing left to say in terms of pain or confusion or troublesome thoughts, and I began to write words of love, of poetry and to draw. Sai Baba still came to me and took the letters, as I knew He would. I cannot really explain why I knew, but I did. My at-one-ment with Him felt so strong to me during that period, His actions could not surprise me.

This daily happening became a ritual at that time for me. So much so, that on one occasion, when I was sitting further to the back and I could not stretch out the letter I had in my hand to Sai Baba, He stopped walking and stood in front of the row I was seated in and waited for my letter. I attempted to stretch the letter out to Him but could not get near Him. Sai Baba asked the lady in front of me to help me, by beckoning to me and saying to her, "Why don't you help her?" He waited patiently as the letter was passed down the row to Him. As I write this I realise how precious those weeks were.

Dearest, Sweetest, Beloved Swami,

As I wrote the above, my heart just filled up with love
at the thought of how patient You were with me at that time,
and how much truly You love me.

Thank You, for showing me the power
and love in writing a letter to God.
You loving daughter,
Mynavati

Sometimes my Guru, Sri Sathya Sai Baba, takes letters from people in Darshan and sometimes He does not. Occasionally, He takes letters from particular people who say that they know that they are to communicate with Him in this way. Others have said to me that they know that they are not to try to give Him letters, as He will not take them.

In my own experience, I have found that there are times when I am to do this with Him and there are times when I am not. For me, my Guru is a manifestation of God, and I am devoted to Him in this way. When it does not seem the "right" time for Sai Baba to take letters from me personally I will still write them to Him as God, and respectfully place them on my altar. In this way I have found my prayers to be read and answered.

Consequently, I have suggested to people that if they are in pain or have a seemingly insurmountable problem to daily write letters to God, to allow their feelings to be expressed until the pain is gone. Often when they do this, they find deeper reasons for the pain and they can also hand this over to God and ease their burdens.

Sometimes, we blame our pain on something that has happened to us or something that someone has done to us, but the truth is that things are rarely that simple. The pain, or the problem is already within us, and this "something" or someone has merely pierced the wound already there and bleeding. As well as my own experience, I have observed people who have followed the process of prayer writing until they have found some resolution, and miracles of healing and love have happened in their lives.

Importantly, when we write our prayer as a letter, we address it to God. It makes a big difference to know that whatever we are saying is formally going "to someone." It makes real the fact that God exists and that we are sending a letter to that Divinity. This helps us to stay more conscious of our prayer, the reality of our situation, and to Whom we are communicating.

I often begin my prayers by writing, "Dear God" or "Beloved Lord." Or, when I feel I wish to particularly address my Guru, I write, "Dearest, Sweetest, Beloved, Swami." I know people who like to address their prayers to the "White Light, Heavenly Father, Great Spirit, or Divine Light." As has been written earlier, our labels of God really do not matter. What matters is to discern which ones feel more right and accessible to us than others and to use the former. It is God who matters.

Finally, most of us like to do something to help ourselves. We like to feel that we have taken an action We like to have tangible evidence of our efforts, something concrete to hold and see. We need this at times. When we put a lot of effort into helping ourselves and we see the result this allows us also to be more open to receiving something in return. For example, if we do a piece of work for someone, we will more likely be open to receiving an expression of their gratitude rather than if we feel we have done nothing. If they offer us something when we have done nothing we might even feel suspicious, or feel that we cannot accept their offer because we do not deserve it.

The mind has many such neuroses and directives. But, in the awareness of them, we can use them to God's advantage. We can play a game, which will satisfy the ego's little neurotic children, and we can reassure them and placate them by giving them something to do. Tell them that, "We are going to write a prayer to God, and this will make us all very special to God, and God will answer us in the most loving way God sees fit." Include these poor little beings of doubt and pain and inadequacy in your heart as you write and pray and watch the miracle of love unfold for them and you. Include all the goodness and what you feel is the badness of you when you unite with God.

There is no one better to go to than God. In going to God we do not need to go in supposed perfection. We meet God with all the aspects of ourselves that we accept and which feel unacceptable to us. There is no One more equipped to understand you, Who loves you and will accept you, more than God? So, Who better to pray to, to depend on, and to write to, to love, to adore, and to share the myriad aspects of yourself than God? Only God can do.

Following my letter-writing weeks with Sai Baba in Kodaikanal, I was blessed with an interview by Him just before my departure for home:

Trouble is a Bubble

When I entered the small interview room attached to Swami's house, I had no idea that my heart had been so opened up to Him through the letter writing. I sat on the floor while Sai Baba talked to some others in the room that He had also called. Swami then came and stood in front of me with a tremendously loving look upon His face.

During the previous months, I had gone through quite a lot of trauma, and had even been examined for a tumour in my throat following a previous interview I had received from Sai Baba three months before. The doctor said that he had seen cases like this before and that they were "a result of shock." What I never told the doctor was that during my first interview with The Avatar (God on Earth in human form) around three months before, and which was my first one, I had a profound experience. When I first looked into Swami's eyes, as I entered the room, I intuited a voice within me saying, "Oh, God, you have met your death."

So, I now understand that this death will be the death of my ego. And, I was aware of knowing this then also. But, the immediate shock to my ego was so immense that it literally formed a lump in my throat. By the way, this tumour caused by shock quickly disappeared after my second interview. I had also been having heart palpitations and this was another health concern. However, the palpitations also ceased shortly afterwards, as a result of Swami's Divine Grace.

As I stared into His dark, fathomless, but immensely loving eyes, Sai Baba asked me, as though He had talked to me only yesterday, "And, how are you now?"

I had thought before that if I had the opportunity to speak with Him again, I would like to ask Him if I was about to die. I had been thinking that this was possible, bearing in mind my recent health problems. I also had many questions, one of them being about all the traumas I had been experiencing since I was last with Him.

But, as I looked into Sai Baba's eyes, I saw many bubbles like the kind children blow out of bubble pipes float in front of me. Each little bubble was filled with a picture of one of my troubles, questions, anxieties and fears. As I was pinned to my Guru's eyes, I became aware that these bubbles were popping all around me. In retrospect, He was telling me that: Trouble is a bubble.

What came out of my heart in that instant shocked me to the core of my being. I had no idea I would ever say the following words to Swami, or even have the courage to say them. The words came from my heart alone and not from my mind. Throughout the entire interview/inner view I had been crying, and yet I found myself saying through the tears and sobs, as if in response to the bubbles bursting as well as to His enquiring how I was now, "It doesn't matter Swami…I just love You." I profoundly realised at that moment that there were no important questions to ask of the Divine. I also realised that all that mattered was that I loved Him—that I loved God!

He replied, "And I love you too."

In conclusion, I believe that the power of writing letters to God is infinite and that this form of prayer can work the miracle of opening the heart. Once the heart is opened, all things are possible.

The following is an example of a letter that Bhagawan Sri Sathya Sai Baba sent to students at one of His colleges. And, this shows how God can also speak to us so tenderly in written prayer:

My Dears !

The time will come when the whole of this dream will vanish. To everyone of us there must come a time when the whole universe will be found to have been a mere dream, when we shall find that the soul is infinitely better than its surroundings. In this struggle through what we call environments, there will come a time when we shall find that these environments were almost zero in comparison with the Power of the Soul. It is only a question of time, and time is nothing in the infinite. It is a drop in the ocean. We can afford to wait and be calm.

With Blessings,
Baba

Prayer in Action and Service to God

6

Some desires to serve God come upon me with impulses so strong I don't know how to exaggerate them... This occurs without reflection; but in an instant it changes me completely, and I don't know where I get so much strength.

Saint Teresa of Avila

We do not have to try to save the world to be of service to God. In fact, if we attempt to do things on a grand scale we usually end up creating a mess, after having inflated our egos, thinking that we are saviors, that we are indispensable and often harming those we went out to save. At the very least, we might get disillusioned and drained.

In my years involved in healing and the teaching of healing techniques, I have seen many instances of this kind of scenario. People suddenly find that they have something to give, such as spiritual healing, which in itself is truly wonderful. But then they impose that "gift" on everyone they come into contact with, whether these people want it or not. They forget that everything is God's responsibility and not their responsibility. When there is appropriateness and it is God's will there is no need to force anything. Something happens perfectly and naturally without anyone having to impose. This can be a pretty subtle happening, and we can all easily fall into the trap of being the "answer" if not the Messiah! We forget God's intrinsic role and wisdom in the Divine Drama, and that God is the Producer, Writer and Director. We are merely actors who need to play our parts well, with enthusiasm, discernment, humility and understanding.

All the time, these self-appointed, saviors think that they are the "doers" and then when their doing fails they cannot understand it, and they subsequently become depressed, drained and even ill themselves.

They did not leave it up to God
and just allow themselves to be
used as pure instruments
of God's Will.

Do-gooders can do a lot of harm!

What is essential in any prayer in action or service to God is our motivation and our humility. Do we do something good, hoping that someone else will recognize our spiritual goodness or that the recipient of our goodness shows us gratitude? There is the wise saying in the Bible, which tells us not to,

let the left hand know what the right hand is doing.

There is a reason for this. Once we let anyone know how good we are in doing something, whatever goodness was possible is spoiled by pride, and the result is that we are arrogant and pompous.

Another phenomenon, which can take place when people first become spiritually inspired, is to just give and give without any discrimination. Sometimes they give so much away that they have nothing left to live on themselves. Common sense alone tells us that this is not really a good thing to do for either the proposed recipients or ourselves. And, again we can create more harm than good.

Spiritual discipline involves mindfulness, awareness of one's actions and the taking of responsibility for one's actions. What good is a prayer in action if there is no awareness or commitment to it or its subsequent effect?

Someone with whom I have been a friend for many years told me recently how overwhelmed and helpless she felt about what was happening in the world. This was affecting her so much that her health was reflecting her anxiety, and she could not sleep well. She is a truly, kind-hearted and compassionate person and like, Avalokiteshvara, the Buddha of Compassion, she was beginning to feel the grief of the relentlessness of human suffering and her inability to do anything about it.

She lives in the UK and most probably like in many affluent Western countries, she was also daily being inundated by begging letters from charitable organisations. These letters portray startling and poignant scenes and heart-rending stories of children, old people, animals, the homeless and so on. She felt overwhelmed. But since she has very little money herself, she could not send anything as a donation. As well as this, she did not feel that she could really *do anything* useful to help.

We talked about this at length. Subsequently, I found myself also contemplating the issues of suffering, helplessness and service. I will share with you now some of what I discovered.

We have our own backyard of life. We have our own spiritual and material commitments to our self, family, friends, work, problems and pertinent things to attend to. These should be our priority responsibilities. For example, what good is it if a man leaves his wife, his responsibilities to her, and to their home, to go off and do some "service" for God by helping strangers? Can God really be satisfied or happy with this? What about the mess and trouble the husband has left behind him through his running off "to do good?" Even if the work is for a good cause, its very foundations are being tilled on stolen earth and can come to no good.

So, God has a way of planning our day with responsibilities and commitments which need attending to and which are necessary to help us to help Divinity in the ways we can. Usually, God puts these "service projects" right under our noses and plants them right on our doorsteps. Sometimes they do not seem as glamorous as the spiritual work others might be doing. For instance, a daughter looking after her aged mother may resent this and see this as an obstruction to her spiritual desire to travel to Africa and help some tribes with AIDS! But, the looking after the aged mother who needs her is as important to God as the tribes in Africa with AIDS. So, indeed,

Charity begins at Home.

And then, do we really need to do something seemingly glamorous, or on a huge scale, or involving a lot of money to please God? What about further following the motto of *Charity begins at Home.* Home can also be our self. We need to take responsibility for the helping and growing of our self as a child or Divine aspect of God. We need to do our homework and lessons.

If everyone in the world took a commitment to try not to follow his or her negative minds and do one good thing a day, if say only a prayer, the world would be a better place. If each day, you decided to grow up a little for God and did as God tells you, God would have at least one person less to deal with that day! There would be at least one person less in the world causing the entire Cosmos trouble.

Even if you cannot find anything externally *good* to do, it is enough that you attempt to take the responsibility of your own thoughts and subsequent actions. It is a huge offering if you even take out five minutes from your usual jam-packed routine full of tasks and priorities and think of God for those few minutes. That's five minutes less pressure on God! That means five minutes less pressure on the entire human race, the Earth, the Cosmos, and beyond. That is, *you* lessen the tension on creation for at least five minutes. I feel that this is service to God. I feel that this is prayer in action.

Every time you observe yourself and take responsibility, attempt to try harder, do not dump your anger, jealousy or negativity on your loved ones or others, you are doing the greatest service to God, and you are saying the most profound prayer in action.

Little Daily Offerings of Prayer in Action to God

It has been said before that we have got into the habit of forgetting God. Just as easily, we can reverse this process and get into the habit of never forgetting God by allowing God to receive all that we do each day.

For example, when you make a cup of tea for someone, make it for God, Divinity. God is within each of us and so to even make a cup of tea for someone is to serve God. Whenever I remember God in making a cup of tea or in cooking some food for guests, they always comment, "This is so delicious." Or they say, "What did you do — How did you make that?" The ingredients may have been simple. They usually are. Often when I prepare food or drinks I chant a favourite mantra or sing a Bhajan (spiritual song). But always the main ingredient in my recipes is: *A Big tablespoon of God.*

Then other times on certain days, I like to cook some food just for God. I make sweet rice, because I believe that God likes sweet rice. I have God's own special dish and cup which is never used for anyone else but God, and I dare not taste the finished product until God has been served. I mix ghee, jaggery, milk, sometimes cream and raisins and rice and make a delicious sweet, which I then serve and place on my altar. After some time, perhaps at the end of the day I give this to some stray dogs near my rooms. Sai Baba has said, "Dog is God." And so I gratefully give these mirror images of God my offering.

I have watched these stray dogs, one in particular named Ramu, who now looks out for me on these special days. Ramu relishes this sweet like no other food. I feel that he recognises the Divine taste of God's blessing and the special intention in the cooking of it. I feel his deep appreciation.

Everything you do can be offered to God. Everything you do can be a prayer to God. It is just a matter of remembering God before you do it and after you do it. It is only a matter of including God and then everything you do in this way is a prayer in service and in action to God.

Here is a true story, related to me personally by two monks of how God appreciates being served in this way:

Leela Tea

One day Sai Baba asked an elderly woman in Darshan about these two monks. She knew them, and He told her to give them a message to come and see Him in Prashanti Nilayam.

The monks had never been to see Sai Baba before. In fact, they had only recently heard of Him. They had been thinking that they would like to visit Him and how to do this, and so they were thrilled to be so personally invited by Sai Baba.

When they arrived in Prashanti, it was almost time for Darshan. The elderly lady, who Sai Baba had asked to invite the monks, had instructed them to come to her apartment first. She wanted to show them where to go and what to do. They arrived at her door, travel weary and thirsty after a hot, long journey from Bangalore on a bumpy government bus.

The lady wished to give them some hospitality by offering them some tea before going to Darshan. Now, this lady was in the habit of always serving God first in anything she did. For example, when she made a cup of tea, she would first pour some in a cup for God and place it on her altar in front of Sai Baba's picture. Only then, would she drink her own tea. Often, apparently, the tea or food that she offered in this way disappeared or lessened in its quantity.

On this day, she made the tea for the two monks. As was usual, she first offered a cup of tea to God, and then one to the monks. They all drank the delicious hot, sweet and refreshing tea. They finished and prepared to leave for Darshan. But, just before they left the room the elderly devotee made an exclamation in surprise.

All the time, the gas cylinder had been disconnected to the stove. There had been no gas that morning and she had waited for a refill. She assumed that the new gas cylinder had come while she was out and had been connected, but in actuality it had not! All three of them tried connecting the cylinder to the stove and found that there was no gas in it at all.

God's Leelas are infinite !

God, in compassion, had provided the gas for the tea for all of them. Surely, this was God's way of thanking the elderly devotee for the cups of tea she gave as a daily offering.

Last, but not least, is the way we can offer a thank you to God for the food that we eat. I remember that this was something I experienced in childhood as part of Christian life and schooling, and how much more commonplace it was then than it is now. It was a little offering, a thank you to God, at least three times a day—the saying of *Grace* before meals. It was a nice experience, that I found comforting. And, it felt good because we remembered God and we gave thanks for the blessing of the food that God provided. In this way, we at least did not forget God at mealtimes.

I remember the children at the school dinner hall, sitting still, with hands together in prayer, and the silence that came just before the saying of *Grace*. Then as soon as *Grace* was [illegible] everyone tucked in as fast as possible, and then God was completely forgotten.

Not long ago, when I was contemplating on the custom of the saying of *Grace,* I realised that this was the only difference between animals and human beings when we eat. In fact, it is the only difference between animals and us in all the things that we do, the way that we satisfy our bodies and desires. That is, we can consciously say thank you to God and hand over even the *fruits* of the entire experience to God as an offering. We are *graced* because we can do this. When we do not use this God-given gift, our human bodies are wasted and we are merely living on the animal level.

Every culture has a way of saying thank you to God for food. The American Indians honour the food they kill, prepare and eat by acknowledging its Divinity, its at-one-ment with the Source. The Hindus chant a *Grace* that honours everything as God, including the food. The following stanzas are from the *Bhagavad Gita,* and are sung in Sai Baba's ashram, Prashanti Nilayam :

Brahmaarpanam Brahma Havihir
Brahmaagnow Brahmanaahutam
Brahmaiyva Thena Ganthavayam
Brahmakarma Samaadhinaa

Aham Vaishuvaanaro Bhootwa
Praninaam Dehamaasrithaha
Praanaapaana Samaayuktaha
Pachaamyannam Chaturvidham.

This essentially means:

The whole creation is a projection of Bramhan,
Who is the Cosmic Consciousness Itself (God).
the food which is also part of this projection is also God.
ffering of the food is therefore God.
ing is to the fire of God
reaches God.

I, the Supreme Spirit,
Abiding in the body of living beings
As the Fire in their stomach,
Digest the four types of food
Which they eat.

Here, we have Divinity, eating Divinity, through the means of Divinity, for the sake of Divinity. The taking of food with this Divine awareness therefore, like all actions, can be a tremendous spiritual exercise and meditation. But now in our fast-increasing blindness of the God-given life, this awareness in action has become more of a rarity.

Now, I do find that I see many people saying *Grace* as a natural part of life in an ashram setting. But, it has become so far-removed from our working, normal, day-to-day lives that if someone said *Grace* at lunchtime in an office canteen in the UK, they would be stared at, and most probably thought of as a fanatic, weird or ridiculous. It might be the same in many schools. However, like most ancient spiritual customs, there are usually pretty basic sound and sensible reasons for doing them. The saying of *Grace* is no exception.

Everything has a vibration, including the food that we eat. The composition of the food has a vibration as well as the seller of the food, the cook, and the place where the food has been kept and so on. When we eat food, say, in a restaurant, we get vibrations from the chairs we sit on and the table we sit at, as well as all the items of cutlery, dishes and so on. When we eat the food, we consume not only the food itself, but also the vibrations from the food, where it was grown, the lorry and drivers that delivered it to the shop, the shopkeeper who handled it, the cook and the server…

This is why we should also say *Grace.* We do so to purify the food and to allow God, the Divine, to bless the food to eradicate any negative vibrational energy from it. One of my favourite, old stories from India tells about this very nicely:

You are What You Eat

There was a good and spiritually inclined kin[illegible] man in his kingdom. The holy man wa[illegible] need for things of the world, and in fact lived in a cave on the outskirts of the Kingdom. But the King respected this old man very much and was happy that he chose to live in his Kingdom.

The King wished to honour the holy man and continually asked the saint to come to his palace for dinner. The King knew that the holy man did not normally eat very much, and even this was simple, plain food. But the King wanted to make him happy by giving him a sumptuous meal. The holy man refused and refused, until one day he gave in and agreed to come to the palace to eat. The King was so happy, as he felt it a great honour that the saint would visit him.

They had a wonderful banquet, and the King made sure that all his best gold and silver tableware and cutlery was laid out on the table in respect of the holy man. They ate together and talked late into the night. The King took the opportunity to ask the holy man many spiritual questions. He asked his guest to stay the night. But the holy man refused and returned to his simple cave.

In the morning, it was found that all the gold and silver tableware was gone. It had been stolen. The King accused his servants, but they insisted that the thief had been the holy man. The King could not believe this story. How could this be when he was a saint? How could this unworldly, holy man steal his gold and silver tableware?

The King visited the holy man in his cave that very day and asked him outright if he had stolen his gold and silver. The holy man said, "Yes, of course, I stole the items. I came back to the palace while you all slept and I took them." And then the saint proceeded to show the King all that he had taken during the night, and which was now in his cave.

The King was shocked. This man he revered and thought of as a
...he listened to for words of wisdom and guidance, was a thief
...d it. He screamed at the holy man, "How could you
...ise of a holy man? You come to my palace as
...How could you do such an atrocious

... thief. He has stolen
...t he cooked I

was so overcome by his energy that I could not resist stealing from you also."

So, the moral of this little story is to say *Grace*, even a silent short *thank you*, before eating, and then you will be safe to eat anywhere without taking on alien vibrations. You will only have God's vibrations in your food!

In finishing this section, I would like to share one of my favorite prayers in action, written by Sai Baba.

Oh Lord,
Take my love and let it flow
in fullness of Devotion to Thee.

Oh Lord,
Take my hands and let them
work Incessantly for Thee.

Oh Lord,
Take my soul and let it be
Merged in one with Thee.

Oh Lord,
Take my mind and thoughts
And let them be in Tune with Thee.

Oh Lord,
Take my everything and let me be
An Instrument to work for Thee.

Prayer through Song, Chant and Mantra

7

Spiritual chanting, singing and repetitive sacred sounds remove us from the distractions of our minds. Such sounds and their evocativeness and beauty can mirror our deepest noble feelings and help us to connect to the Divine. Spiritual sound can stir our souls and ignite our hearts. It can move us to tears and at the point of crying we are not even interested in what our minds have to say. What happens is that we merge the mind with the sound and the mind is pacified and healed with the Divine Love emanating from the vibrations. We are elevated to a higher plane and beyond.

History indicates that human beings of all cultures and creeds have sung praises to the Creator, composed from the love in their hearts. Hymns, chants mantras, Aums and Bhajans have circled the world for centuries expressing humankind's longing for union with God.

Devotional Song

Love is My Form,
Truth is My Breath,
Bliss is My Food,
My Life is My Message,
Expansion is My Life,
No Reason for Love,
No Season for Love,
No Birth, No Death.

Song of Divinity by Sri Sathya Sai Baba

Sri Ramakrishna, the famous Indian Saint who died in 1886, often burst into song and danced in ecstasy for his God, most frequently in the aspect of the Divine Mother. As a young priest, when Sri Ramakrishna's love for God deepened, it is said that he either dropped or forgot the formalities of worship. Sitting before the image of the Divine Mother, he would spend hours singing songs composed by Her great devotees. These songs described the experience of the direct vision of God. This singing intensified Sri Ramakrishna's longing for God so much, that in agony, he would rub his face against the ground and weep bitterly. On seeing him, people would think that he had lost his earthly mother and would sympathise with him in his grief. Obviously, he really did feel the pangs of a child bereft of its mother, and before long his intense desire brought to him the vision he so much wanted.

As it happened, one night he thought he could not bear the separation from his God any longer. Later, he related the following story:

I was determined to end my life. When I jumped up like a madman and seized it, (a sword kept in the Divine Mother's temple), suddenly the Blessed Mother revealed herself. The buildings with their different parts, the temple, and everything else vanished from my sight, leaving no trace whatsoever, and in their stead I saw a limitless, infinite, effulgent Ocean of Consciousness. As far as the eye could see, the shining billows were madly rushing at me from all sides with a terrific noise to swallow me up! I was panting for breath. I was caught in the rush and collapsed, unconscious. What was happening in the outside world I did not know; but within me there was a steady flow of undiluted bliss, altogether new, and I felt the presence of the Divine Mother.

I recall a dream I had sometime after I met my own Guru, Sai Baba:

Sai Baba was seated on a chair and I sat on the floor in front of Him. As I looked at Him, there began to well up within me an intense feeling of love and devotion. The strength of the feeling was so overwhelming that I lost any sense of self. Energy travelled upwards through my body and it emerged as the most Divine and poignant sound. The sound was a manifestation of my devotion and love. As this sound came through me, I lifted my arms in ecstasy and my face towards the heavens. Wet, clean snowflakes fell gently upon me. Tears welled up with the sound and I awoke feeling like an open flower.

When we love so much, when we feel so much devotion, words are sometimes not enough, and pure sound or a sound filled with emotion can say much more.

Sai Baba says:

Do you know why you have been given your mouth? Is it to utter all kinds of words? No, it has been given to you so that you might sing the Glory of the Lord.

Swami is a great advocate of congregational singing and in Prashanti Nilayam where we attend His Darshan, Bhajans are sung each morning and evening.

It has been my experience that whenever I have sung devotional songs, either alone or in a gathering, I have, during and on finishing, felt so much more happy and connected to God. It is that simple. There have been times when I have felt a resistance to singing, especially if I have been feeling unwell or emotionally low. But then, if I can just break the barrier of the defence and sing, my whole world changes and I become much more optimistic and elevated.

I have noticed the same thing in my work with people, primarily during the retreats and workshops where we often sing and chant. Some people find that they cannot open their mouths to take that initial step of just letting go to the sound and to sing. They say that they feel self-conscious or they have had a particularly bad experience as a child, being told perhaps that they could not sing.

Actually, one cannot push these things. There is a time that is appropriate for each of us to open up to sacred sound. But I have been privileged and felt thrilled to see, when these people do finally let go of their hesitation and sing, the transformation is so obvious. It shows on their faces. In fact, their entire being radiates with joy. It is as though a Divine light has been switched on within them, and they just shine.

It is true that some people cannot sing very well in harmony, or they sing out of tune. But, this need not be a problem. We do not have to be accomplished singers to sing to the Divine. If we chant

"Aum" or "Amen" or any sound we feel drawn to and fuel this with the love-fire of our heart, our sounds will be Divine, and we will immediately be connected to Divinity.

Sai Baba tells us to spiritualise our singing:

What is required is transformation of the heart. All bad thoughts and feelings should be expelled from the heart. Even in the performance of Bhajans there should be whole-hearted participation in them. It should not be a mechanical ritual. Once your heart is filled with sacred thoughts and feelings, they will be reflected in your Bhajan-singing. Through your singing you should give joy to all the participants.

Swami refers in particular to the singing of Bhajans here, but of course His words are relevant for all devotional singing. Even if there is only you present to the sound of your own voice, the aim in singing is to give joy to you and everything and everyone. For me, devotional singing is the sound of prayer filled with joyous and heavenly vibrations. These vibrations radiate to the entire Earth and beyond. Everyone and everything is inspired by another's connection to Divinity, no matter how seemingly far away they are in time, space and consciousness. The ultimate result of sacred sound uttered as intense prayer is that the singer, the chanter, has the potential to become one with God and in this oneness becomes Who they really are.

Swami Rama Tirtha, an ecstatic saint of India, (1873-1906) is one of my favourite writers of devotional songs. The following hymn came from the book of his collected songs and poetry, *Songs of Enlightenment:*

Know for certain that you yourself are God,
The Supreme Self, the eye of the eye,
Which the eye cannot see.
You are the essence of speech,
Which speech cannot express.
You are the hearer of hearing,
Which the ear cannot hear.

You are the life of life,
Who does not need the life-force to live,
Recognise that you are the light of mind,
Which the mind cannot know...

You do not need to be a saint to sing your song to God. You can write your own expression of love as a song and sing the words whenever you wish, or you can improvise as and whenever you feel. Our words do not need to be sophisticated but can be like those of a child. Once, when I was living in Lucknow near the abode of the Guru Poonjaji, who was a Self-Realised disciple of Bhagavan Sri Ramana Maharishi, I was moved by hearing one of his devotees sing a simple Western song with profound lyrics that are often overlooked:

Row, row, row, your boat
Gently down the stream
Merrily, merrily, merrily, merrily
Life is but a dream.

Mantras and Chanting

Mantras and chanting are sacred sounds sung in repetition. They emit vibrations of immense power. As in singing Bhajans, when chanting mantras, a person's entire energy field will change. Where there is darkness, light will manifest, and where there are blocked residual energies in someone's field of subtle energy (The Aura), due to negative thoughts and anxieties, chanting will purify. I have personally been witness to how miracles can happen when chanting mantras

My first introduction to a Tibetan Buddhist mantra was some time in 1990-91. My dear friend Eve, a Tibetan Buddhist practitioner, introduced me to the mantra. I recall that she gave me a picture of Guru Rinpoche, the Deity the mantra evoked and celebrated, with the mantra written below. I asked Eve how to pronounce the words correctly and she sang it for me. I remember that as I heard her sing the mantra, something just stirred in my being, like recognition and a desire to chant the mantra too. And so I learned the mantra myself and I chanted it almost constantly. I chanted it while I did household chores, before I went to sleep, and internally while I worked as a healer with patients. The mantra became very much part of my life. At that time, I did no other meditation or spiritual practices. I chanted the mantra out of a love for the mantra itself and with no thought as to what it could do for me although Eve had told that it was considered to be a powerful mantra for the "Removal of Obstacles."

The mantra was called the *Guru Rinpoche Mantra*. It is the mantra of Padmasambhava, and in Tibetan Buddhism it is thought of as the mantra of all the Buddhas, Masters and Realised Beings. Padmasambhava brought the Buddhist teachings to Tibet from India. It is said that as Buddha was Himself passing away, He prophesied the coming of Padmasambhava not long after His death. Padmasamhava's role was to teach the Path to Liberation through Tantra (The Mystical and Magical Path of Spiritual Energy, rather than the Buddha's Path of Renunciation).

This came about and Padmasambhava established Buddhism in Tibet in the eighth century. Padmasambhava is said to have spontaneously manifested as an eight-year-old boy sitting on a lotus flower in the middle of a lake in Oddiyana. Because of this miraculous birth, He was known as the *lotus born.* His name comes from the Sanskrit words *padma* meaning *lotus* and *sambhava* meaning *born.*

Within two years of chanting this mantra, my life drastically changed and after a series of miraculous happenings, I found myself in India for the first time staying in a Tibetan Rinpoche's home in Sikkim, (A Principality of India) in the Himalayas for a period of almost six months. I say "found myself" for I had had no prior ambition to visit India. But everything happened in such a way to make it all incredibly easy for me, even to the meeting of the Rinpoche in Edinburgh, Scotland.

When I was in Sikkim, I discovered that everywhere I went I was walking on the ground that Guru Rinpoche walked. This was land that He had travelled and where He had taught and everyone I met seemed to be chanting this mantra. I realised then how my chanting of this mantra was fulfilling itself in such a miraculous way.

On another occasion, years later, I was with my husband travelling in our jeep through the night from a place in India called Gokarna to Kerala. Again, a miraculous happening occurred in connection with chanting a mantra. This time it was with the *Gayatri Mantra*, one of the most ancient, powerful and sacred Hindu mantras chanted today.

The Power of the Gayatri Mantra

It was around three a.m. in the morning. My husband, Sudevan, and I had stopped for diesel in a petrol station we had found on the way. It was the month of March when the summer heat is most intense. Even at that time of night the air was hot. Everything seemed incredibly still and quiet, and there was no sign of anyone on the road. Not long after we had filled the jeep up with the diesel, there was in unseasonable slight mist of rain. We came to a small, curving bridge and as we drove on it we suddenly began to skid on the hot, but now slimy wet road. After moving from one side to the other a few times, we then hit one of the little white round stone barriers at the edge and began to topple over the side. We looked at each other, both of us thinking that this was the end. We had no idea what was at the bottom, how deep the drop was. We turned upside down and fell with a heavy crash. Luckily, we landed on dry ground--the river had dried up. In India, seat belts are generally not used because they do not necessarily work.

But, for some reason I had put the safety belt on around 30 minutes before the crash.

The whole top of the jeep was crushed, but somehow we were still alive. Sudevan managed to get out and then began to help me out. Although the safety belt had saved me from hitting the windscreen or from flying through the air, I was stuck and there seemed an interminable time before I was loosened. At the same time, nearby villagers, on hearing the crash sounds, had come running to help and they were shouting, "Diesel! Diesel!" I knew what was happening, that the diesel was coming out of the tank. I now imagined during that seemingly long expansion of time that although I had survived the crash, my fate was that I was going to burn to death. By some miracle, although the air and road was stiflingly hot, the full tank of diesel did not ignite as it flowed from the jeep.

My husband was moving about and seemed okay but I had no idea of the extent of my injuries until I managed to get out of the jeep. Miraculously we were both all right. The jeep was lying crumpled, upside down, but we only had bruising and shock. Nothing was broken and there was no permanent damage. However, I had a bruised collar bone which took quite a long time to heal, and, as a result, I could not sleep on my left side for a year. I had a black eye with an enormous lump above it. My husband was bruised and shaken.

A couple of weeks before we had stayed in Puttapurti at Sai Baba's Ashram, for the Shiva festival of Mahashivaratri. There, we had purchased a small car sticker of Sai Baba, and we had placed it on the windscreen of our jeep. When we both got out of the wreckage, we saw that the front windscreen of the jeep with Sai Baba's sticker photo on it had slid out onto the ground in front of the smashed vehicle all in one piece and without a scratch. We then noticed that we were each holding a small photograph of Sai Baba also. We had no recollection of how or when we had reached for the photographs, or if we had, indeed, done that. We think that we may have had some photos of Sai Baba in our bags near the front of the jeep. But to this day, I am still not sure if those photographs that appeared in our hands were the ones in the bags. And, if they were, how did they get into our hands ?

Later, as we talked about the incident, Sudevan and I were stunned to share with each other that we had both began to chant the ***Gayatri Mantra*** *internally about 10 minutes before the crash. Unknown to the other, each had been doing so intermittently, throughout the evening and night. I am convinced that the* ***Gayatri Mantra*** *and its connection to Divinity, (for us, the presence of Sai Baba) saved our lives.*

The jeep had to lie in the ravine for a few days before we could get it moved. During that time, the local police, who were extremely helpful, stood guard over the vehicle and our belongings within it.

They told us that people in cars stopped on the way to look at the scene and to ask who and how many people had been killed. The police happily told them no one died and that there were two people who were now in a nearby hotel. The curious passers by heard this in absolute disbelief. They could not imagine how anyone survived. The villagers, the police, and the travellers passing by all thought that it was a miracle. So did we. *This is the power of a mantra and its connection to The Divine, to God.*

By definition, a mantra is "that which protects the mind." A mantra protects us from our negative thoughts and the mind from its own negativity. This protection is called mantra. Tibetan Buddhism teaches how the mind rides on the subtle energy of the breath, which moves through the subtle channels of the body. When we chant a mantra, we are able to charge these subtle fields with the Divine energy of the mantra. My own experience in the jeep crash reveals to me how a mantra can protect us physically as well as mentally. Of course, our minds and bodies are completely related, so how could they not both be protected? To change the energy of the mind is to change everything that is manifested by the mind.

Hindu Scripture teaches that the OM sound is the sound of the Universe that includes all sounds. The OM sound vibrates and vitalises every atom and it energises, sustains and fills the Cosmos. We ourselves are OM, just as everything is a manifestation of OM. To chant the OM is to chant oneself and allow one's Divinity to manifest.

When I lead retreats and workshops, I usually include the chanting of at least 21 OM sounds. Sometimes people are so impressed by the power and beauty of the chanting and of how it helps them so easily to connect to Divinity that they continue to chant the OM as part of their daily spiritual practice. I recommend that they do this after waking up in the morning, and they find that in doing so they feel strengthened in body, mind and spirit and they are better able to meet the challenges of the day.

There is something profoundly significant in chanting a mantra 21 times. The reason is that we have five outer senses, five inner senses, five elements and five sheaths, altogether totalling 20. The recitation of OM 21 times purifies and clarifies all these 20 components and makes the chanter the 21st entity, ready for the final merger with Reality. I usually chant a mantra at least 21 times, and I repeat the mantra as a series 21 times.

There is no limit to how many times one might chant a mantra. But, traditionally, people usually chant a mantra 108 times. If one buys a mantra malla, (a type of rosary) it should contain 108 beads with one extra "Guru" bead at the top end of the malla. This bead represents the presence of the Guru. If this is helpful to you, then you could do your chanting using your malla as a tool. But repetition is not so important as feeling and meaning. Sometimes people can get so easily caught up in the counting of the mantra that they lose any real connection to the chanting of it.

There is a story of how once a boy was given the ***Gayatri Mantra*** *to recite by his father. He was asked to recite it in the traditional way, repeating it 108 times. Soon, the father noticed that the boy was finishing his task very quickly. He was puzzled. Then after some investigation, the father found that the boy was saying the mantra once, and then repeating, "Likewise... Likewise... Likewise, 107 times!*

We may not exactly say, "Likewise," when we have such a task in hand, but if we let the mind take over with its agenda of irrelevant thoughts and abandon any real connection to what we are chanting, we are as good as saying, "Likewise."

You may find it interesting to take note that repetitive chanting forms patterns that help to change our brainwaves. Changing brainwaves break "concrete" thought patterns, thoughts that can hold tension-giving emotions and attitudes. Chanting mantras is, therefore, a very powerful tool for helping us to break free of our usual way of being and our conditioning. In the process of breaking free of our conditioning, we can transform. The less that our minds rule us, the more we know and connect to the wisdom and compassion of our Divine hearts.

It is also understood that, as we chant mantras, the roofs of our mouths change their shape. The mouth is like a temple and is perfectly shaped to accommodate and reverberate sound. Sound strikes the pineal and pituitary glands as it moves like a wave around the internal dome of your mouth. The Crown and Brow Chakras control the pineal and pituitary glands, respectively. In chanting mantras, we activate The Crown and Brow Chakras and we can open up more intuitively and spiritually.

As the words of mantras have been chosen for their sound and its effect, as well as for their meaning, it is important that you have perfect pronunciation of them. The alphabet of the Sanskrit language is endowed with special vibrational powers. When theses sounds are uttered in specific esoteric combination this produces sacred and Divine sound waves with tremendous vibrations which affect the entire planet. For this reason, mantras should always be chanted in their original Sanskrit form and not translated, as they will lose their particular sound waves and frequencies.

The following are a selection of some well-known chants and their meanings. I have also attempted to help with the phonetic pronunciation of the sounds. However, there is nothing better than to hear them being chanted by someone who is proficient. There are also now many CDs and cassettes available with the mantras chanted on them. (Our CD or tape cassette which includes the following mantras, can we ordered by contacting, e-mail: cosmic power press@yahoo.co.in)

Well-Known Chants/Mantras

OM

Pronounced as:

Ohm

Om signifies the original primordial sound. Everything that has manifested in the Cosmos has come from this sound. Sound gives rise to vibrations and vibrations give rise to movement. The sound caused by creation gave rise to the movement of the entire Cosmos.

We have come from this sound, and so chanting this sound connects us to the very essence of our Being. The A-U-M sound of the OM represents the "Om Tat Sat" principle which is, "I am the Truth."

A good time to chant the sound of OM is in the early hours of the morning. But, at any time of the day it is helpful and healing. Chant a minimum of 21 Oms (per session) each day and you will find a great difference in all your Chakras (psychic energy centres).

My Guru Sri Sathya Sai Baba relates it this way:

Repeat the "AUM" slowly contemplating its vast potentialities.
The "A" emerges from the throat,
"U" rolls over the tongue
and the "M" ends on the lips;
that is to say, OM which is composite of A-U-M
is the sum and substance of all words
which can emanate from the human tongue.
It is the primordial fundamental sound,
symbolic of the Universal Absolute.
After the "M" there must be the unheard resonance,
which represents the attributeless, formless, Abstract,
the Niraakaara Parabrahmam.
The ascending voice of the Pranava or OM
must take a curve at "M" and descend as slowly as it rose,
taking as much time as when it ascended
disappearing in the silence,
which echoes in the inner consciousness.

OM NAMAH SHIVAYAH
(Mantra to Shiva)

Pronounced as:

Ohm Nam Ah Shee vigh yah

Generally meaning:

Chant the name of Shiva. (He is the Lord of Energy Who destroys the fear of the cycle of birth and death. He is the Divine Cosmic Dancer and He is the Destroyer of fear, sin and bondage.)

Chanting this mantra helps to destroy our attachments to that which is temporary and illusory and connects us with That which is Permanent and True.

OM MANI PADME HUM
The Mantra of Compassion (Tibetan Buddhist Chant)

Pronounced as:

Ohm Mah Nee Pahd May Hum

Or, the general Tibetan way

Om Mah Nee Peh May Hum Hrih

This mantra embodies the compassion and blessing of all the Buddhas and Bodhisattvas, (Those realised beings who out of their compassion vow to be reborn again and again to help all creation). This mantra especially invokes Avalokiteshvara, the Buddha of Compassion.

Avalokiteshvara prayed before the Buddhas of the 10 Directions, "*May I help all beings, and if I ever tire in this great work, may my body be shattered into a thousand pieces.*" It is said that he first descended into the hell realms, ascending gradually through the different worlds up to the realms of the Gods. From there, he happened to look down. And, to his great dismay, he saw that though he had saved countless beings from hell, more were pouring in.

When He saw this, Avalokiteshvara experienced the most profound grief, so much grief that, for a moment, he almost lost faith in his vow. In that instant, His body exploded into a thousand pieces. He desperately called out to all the Buddhas for help, and with their power and compassion they made Him whole again. From then on, He is said to have 11 heads and a thousand arms and on each palm of his hands is an eye, signifying the union of wisdom and skilful means which is the essence of true compassion. In His immense power He repeated his vow, "*May I not attain final Buddhahood before all sentient beings attain enlightenment.*"

Explanation of the Six-Syllable OM MA NI PAD ME HUM

OM closes the door to the suffering of being reborn in the ***Gods' Realm.*** *The suffering of the gods arises from foreseeing one's fall from the* ***Gods' Realm.*** *This suffering comes from pride.*

MA closes the door to the suffering of being reborn in the ***Warring Gods' Realm.*** *The suffering of this realm is constant fighting. This suffering comes from jealousy.*

NI closes the door to the suffering of being reborn in the ***Human Realm.*** *The suffering of humans is birth, sickness, old age, and death. This suffering comes from desire.*

PAD closes the door to the suffering of being reborn in the ***Animal Realm.*** *The suffering of animals is stupidity, preying upon one another, being killed by men for meat, skins, etc., and being beasts of burden. This suffering comes from ignorance.*

ME closes the door to the suffering of being reborn in the ***Hungry Ghosts' Realm.*** *The suffering of hungry ghosts is hunger and thirst. This suffering comes from greed.*

HUM closes the door to the suffering of being reborn in the ***Hell Realms.*** *The suffering of the hells is heat and cold. This suffering comes from anger or hatred.*

When we chant the six- syllable mantra, OM MANI PADME HUM, the six negative emotions, which are the root cause of the six realms of suffering, are purified. It is said that if we chant or recite this mantra, we clear our suffering in each realm as well as prevent rebirth in each of the six realms.

THE GURU RINPOCHE MANTRA or VAJRA GURU MANTRA

OM AH HUM VAJRA GURU PADMA SIDDHI HUM

Pronounced as:

Aum Ah Hung Benza Guru Pema Siddhi Hung

Meaning essentially:

I invoke You, the Vajra Guru, Padmasambhava, by Your blessing may You grant us ordinary and supreme siddhis.

The following interpretation is merely an outline, from my understanding of the detailed rendering in *The Tibetan Book of Living and Dying* and the oral explanations given to me from my Tibetan teachers. Although limited, I hope that it will be helpful to you in understanding the basic principles.

The syllables **OM AH HUM** have outer, inner and secret meanings. But at each level,

OM stands for body,

AH for the speech

and

HUM for the mind.

By purifying your body, speech and mind, OM AH HUM grants the blessing of the body, speech and mind of the Buddhas.

VAJRA is compared to the diamond. Just as a diamond can cut through anything, but remains whole, the unchanging, non-dual wisdom of the Buddhas can never be harmed by ignorance and can cut through all delusion and obstacles.

GURU means The Master, someone who embodies wisdom, knowledge, compassion and skilful means.

PADMA means lotus. It signifies the lotus family of the Buddhas to which human beings belong.

When combined together, the syllables *VAJRA GURU PADMA*, mean that we receive the blessing of the wisdom mind, the noble qualities and the compassion of Padmasambhava and all the Buddhas.

SIDDHI means attainment, or real accomplishment. This includes the ordinary accomplishment of the removal of obstacles in our lives such as of ill health etc., and Real Accomplishment is the blessing of complete realisation of Padmasambhava, which is the state of enlightenment itself.

HUM means the wisdom mind of the Buddhas and is the sacred catalyst of the mantra. It is like proclaiming "So be it!" or "It is done!"

THE GAYATRI MANTRA

Aum, Bhur Bhuvah Suvah
Tat Savitur Varenium
Bhargo Devasya Dhimahi
Dhiyo Yo Nah Prachodayat

Pronounced as:

Aum Bhoor Boo Vah Sva Ha
Tat Sah Veet Toor Va Ren Yum
Bar Go Day Vha See Ah Deem Ahee
Dhee Yoh Yoh Nah Pra Show Dye Aht

The *Gayatri Mantra* is one of the oldest mantras recorded. Sai Baba says that it is, in fact, the Mother of the Vedas because it embodies the total Truth of Reality. Gayatri is the Divine Mother, the Feminine Energy of the Cosmos. The mantra honours this force—Shakti Energy, as it dwells in the Sun, (Savitur). The Sun is the symbol of the power of Creation, of the intelligence of Consciousness that resides in all existence. It calls upon the Force to arouse, strengthen and awaken intelligence in all levels of our being. It is our intelligence that leads us to have spiritual strength and discrimination.

Sai Baba says about the meaning of the *Gayatri:*

Aum, Bhur, Bhuvah, Suvah represent the three basic principles of Godliness in everyone. Bhur means matter. Bhuvah is the Prana Shakti (the vibrant principle), Suvah is the Prajna Shakti (awareness). These three constituent forces – radiation, vibration and material energy – activate the human being. But man is not able to realise this fact.

The mantra begins with:

Aum

Which is the primordial sound of the Universe.

It then continues with:

Bhur, Bhuva Suvah,

which is the earth, heaven and the transcendental state, known in Vedic philosophy as the three worlds. They can also be thought of as the physical, mental and psychological levels. But we cannot limit their meaning. They are said to be the words of power by God when God created the Cosmos. Their meaning is therefore infinite and of infinity.

The next lines of the mantra are:

Tat Savitur Varenium
Bhargo Devasya Dhimahi

Here, we call upon Savitur, the most heavenly One. Savitur is the power of the Sun which manifests in the three worlds and which gives *life* to the worlds. This is the evocation of the power, the Sun that is self-luminous Consciousness. ***Bhargo, Devasya Dimahi*** is the radiance of all the Grace, Abundance and Blessings that we can imagine pouring forth from the glorious Savitur.

The remaining line is:

Dhiyo Yo Na Prachodayat

In this final part of the mantra, after our tremendous effort of devotion in placing ourselves in This Wondrous Light, we let go and surrender to the Divine. We realise that we are not the "doer" and the enlightenment of our intellect is ours already even as we ask.

Sai Baba says:

...Therefore, rely on the ***Gayatri*** *to draw down the Effulgence of the Sun so that it may impart Illumination to your intellect.*

Many practitioners of the ***Gayatri*** will repeat the mantra three times a day : Dawn, noon and sunset. They also chant it when bathing to purify the entire being.

There are, of course, mantras and chants from every spiritual and religious tradition. I chose the above ones to share with you, not because I feel that these are any better or have more spiritual worth than others from,say, American Indian Spiritual Chants, but because I personally chant them as prayers and have felt the power, vibration and love inherent in them.

Silence

Last, but not least, is the power of the "sound" of Silence. This "sound" contains the preciousness of internal silence and of external silence.

We are almost constantly bombarded externally by background noise, chatter garish music and songs. We have become so accustomed to these mundane sounds that we seem to have become outwardly anaesthetised, unaware, or unperturbed by them.

Whether we are consciously aware of it or not, this cacophony stresses our beings on every level and creates additional tension and distraction. You can experiment with this yourself. Turn on a fan or dehumidifier, or anything which has an ongoing, background, droning-type sound. Leave it on until you forget that you hear it. Set an alarm to ring a few hours later and at that time turn the switch off. Now, register how you feel without the background noise. I have experienced this and felt the most tremendous relief in just not having that noise! And yet when it was making a sound, I had become so used to it that I was not even registering it. I had become so accustomed to the resultant stress that I was not aware of it and how it was affecting my body, mind and spirit.

People live in constant seeming oblivion to the background noise of television, radio, stereos, washing machines, spin dryers, construction, traffic, departmental store music and the like. As well as this, we move around with walk-mans planted on our ears, with mobile telephones and beepers that seem to ring incessantly. Immersed in this hullabaloo, how can we even begin to remember that we are human beings, to be able to inwardly contemplate on any level, let alone pray? Along with this disquiet and everyone else's noise, we ourselves sometimes never stop talking, blasting, shouting or trumpeting.

Sri Sathya Sai Baba says:

You feel the presence of God
when silence reigns...
That is why I insist on silence,
the practise of low speech
and
minimum sound.
Talk low,
talk little,
talk in whispers,
sweet and true.

Apart from the external distractions of our own and others' irrelevant and painful noises, there is the ruthlessly ongoing internal distraction of our own thoughts, the blabbing of constant memories, projections of the future, desires and dislikes.

The important thing here is to be aware of this multifarious internal noise. That way it cannot do the bidding of its secret and poisonous cover up of your heart. Watch these negative vibrations as they arise. Do not follow them, and they will dissolve. Let them be, have pity on them, but do not constantly give them your attention and precious life energy. In accomplishing this, you will be the recipient of the treasure of moments of silence and its unerring, unspoken prayer.

The following is a spontaneous prayer that came to me while writing this section:

In the true silence of the mind,
when the thoughts fade away
and, for a moment,
there is the stillness
and, the echo of the nothing,
which contains everything,
the world becomes still.
And I am
aware more than I ever was before.

I am
aware of the sound of moving blades of grass,
of the whispering wind dancing through each stem.

I am
aware of the sound of each step,
of the beetle's foot upon the ground.
All the sounds I hear are Divine.

And in this,
I hear the sound of You,
my Dear God,
and I feel
at one
with Thy Own Self
in the heartbeat of this offering,
my silent prayer.

Mynavati

Part 2
Meditation

Helping the Mind to Help You

8

O, Rama, what is done by the mind alone is action; and what is abandoned or renounced by the mind alone is renunciation. The mind that has been relieved of its object becomes steady. Then by deep meditation it attains the supreme state. When the mind is properly and effectively disciplined, the world-illusion vanishes.

The Yoga Vasishata—(The Supreme Yoga)

Like prayer, meditation does not need to be confined to pocketed periods in one's day or used only when one feels the dire necessity to find some peace or inner stillness. It can be incorporated into each moment of one's daily life and activities. It need not be something that is a strain or a stress or split from our normal life and routine. With a little bit of understanding, it can be a happy thing to do.

It is impossible to cover the entire spectrum of meditational practices within a book of this size. What is outlined on the following pages is a guide to general meditational procedures for people who want to know more about them and who want to do them at home and as part of their daily devotional life, for example, people who want to pray, meditate and do affirmations in order to be happy.

Those who wish to study meditation in depth and to practice extensively are advised to seek experienced Masters. Please, do not attempt to do advanced meditation techniques such as Vipassana, Kryia Yoga, Pranayama, etc., or sit for long periods in meditation without on-going, expert supervision. To do so puts you at great risk because when you open yourself up in such an isolated, concentrated and deep way, you can seriously affect your mental stability as well as your physical health.

But, aside from these issues, in talking with people about meditation, I have found that they sometimes have various, almost quite frightening, ideas about meditation, and that this puts them off the idea of even trying it as a part of their daily lives. They think, for example, that they may encounter, or even invite ghosts or other kinds of psychic disturbances to them because they are doing this risky thing called meditation. Even some more spiritually educated people, who would scoff at this very idea, think that meditation is a difficult exercise which demands a lot of commitment from them — a commitment which they feel they cannot possibly incorporate in their daily lives because they are so busy. They think that meditation is okay if one is on a spiritual retreat or for people who want to do "that kind of thing," and that it is not practical for "me, because I have to work" or "I am in the real world." What they are really saying is that people who meditate having nothing else to do in life or that they are dropouts.

Some people have told me that they do not meditate because they cannot get up in the morning. Some say, because it makes them feel "different," that they find it difficult to go to work afterwards, so they "need to keep away from that kind of thing." Because people generally see meditation as something they have to "take time out to do," they of course, can never find the time in their busy and hectic world to do it, even though they might really want to. Then, there are people who are just plain idle and do not want to make the effort of having to do something other than the normal things they do.

Just Lazy

I have a friend who told me of a true story of a woman who was very much involved in Yoga exercises and was furthering her study in her Yoga practice. She travelled to India and, as she visited the various Masters she was learning the Yoga from, she asked what was for her a burning question that had been on her mind about why some people do not spiritually progress very quickly, while some other people do. She never quite got a satisfactory answer until she asked a little, old Indian Yoga practitioner in some remote and unheard of place. He beamingly smiled in deep recognition of her question and nodding his head from side to side in true Indian fashion gave her the profound answer, "Lazy, just lazy."

And isn't he right? We are in the habit of not using our minds in a concentrated or focussed way. Rather, we have got used to living with the thoughts of our mind being scattered, disjointed, nonsensical, flighty, habitual and fragmented. Sitting in a cross- legged position for one hour is not going to make any difference to this inclination of our minds. Sitting in this way for five hours will be no better. You will probably end up with a lot of discomfort and body pain, and you will feel irritated and fed-up. What is required of us is concentrated effort and vigilance. But, often we become so lazy and so sleepy that we shy away from the very idea of trying to be wakeful. So, meditation involves work. And we have the job of helping the mind to become more aware, disciplined and concentrated.

By learning how to concentrate, we learn how to control the senses and create the necessary purity of the mind so that the Divine can be experienced. We need the mind in order to focus. We need the mind to do tasks for us. We need its army of thoughts.

But you need to be the Master of your mind and not the mind's slave. Concentration and meditation will help you to do this.

It is not easy to change the habitual life of the mind. It cannot be done with a thought. It has to be done with effort. But even a few seconds a day can make a huge difference. I remember feeling relieved when I first heard and read what my Guru Sai Baba said about concentration and meditation, and this inspired me to know that, although it can be difficult, taken in stages, it is not an insurmountable task.

Sai Baba says:

How is meditation to be done? The first step is concentration. Twelve concentrations amount to one meditation. Twelve meditations equal one samadhi (equal mindedness or complete consciousness). Concentration is steady, concentrated viewing of an object for 12 seconds. You have to look at an object, a flame, a picture, or an idol for 12 seconds with total concentration, without blinking the eyelids. Practising concentration is preparation for meditation. The duration of meditation is 12 concentrations. This means it should last 12 x 12 or 144 seconds, or 2 minutes 24 seconds. Meditation does not call for sitting in meditation for hours. Proper meditation need not last more than 2 minutes and 24 seconds. It is only after concentration has been practised that one can do meditation well.

Twelve meditations equal one samadhi. This means 144 x 12 seconds or 28 minutes and 28 seconds, very much less than an hour. If samadhi is prolonged it may prove fatal.

I first learned of this discovery a few years ago, and as I say, I thought, Wow, I can really do this. I thought that it would be really simple. But, even when I initially tried to concentrate on one thing for 12 seconds, I realised that the discipline of my thoughts was so slack that I could not quite make the 12 seconds required. I always blinked at the eleventh second. The more I tried the worse it got. I realised just how rowdy my mind was. This was quite a shock, and very humbling for me!

But, I am so grateful to have found this out because now I know what is required of me. I am still heading for the attempt of 12 x 12 of one concentration equalling one meditation x 12 to fully experience Sai Baba's method of open-eye meditation.

However, in my experience, it is easier to concentrate with the eyes closed in that you do not have to worry about blinking. On the other hand, as soon as you close your eyes, the thoughts can come like rampant soldiers.

Sai Baba says about another method:

There is also an internal method of practising concentration. When you close your eyes, a small dark spot appears before the inner eye. You may concentrate on this spot for 12 seconds without letting it move. By this practise, the power of meditation can be developed.

Yogis throughout the ages have practised in this way to discipline their minds. As you can now see, this way of practising by focussing the mind on an object is essential because concentration is what stops the thoughts. Sai Baba once told how Ramana Maharishi would stand on his terrace and concentrate on a particular star for 12 seconds. Even a saint such as Ramana Maharishi had to do this. How can we expect to achieve any balance or quiet in our minds without effort? But with practice, effort and vigilance, we can help our mind to work for us rather than against us.

Before Meditation

There is absolutely no point in sitting for hours in meditation to prove a kind of technical performance. At the end of this, we may accomplish some wonderful disciplining of our thoughts and minds, but what is the purpose without contacting God? We need to remember that the whole point of meditation is, first and foremost, to be united with God, with Divinity, with the Buddha Mind or whatever we call our idea of the Force. And so, on sitting down and in any preparation, the first thing we need to do is call on God to be with us.

Now this may seem a very basic and obvious thing to repeat, but as has been said earlier, we have got into the habit of forgetting God, and so we need to remember and get into the habit of including God instead. I have seen many people forget why they are meditating and place the emphasis on the technique. The purpose of meditation is completely forgotten. So, first, God !

This honouring and inclusion can be done in any way, choosing any form that you feel good with. Think about it like this, that if you want someone to come and join you for tea you will formally invite him or her to come. It would be very rude to be offhand about it, and if you forget to invite them and assume that they will just come along, you will end up being very disappointed.

So, why not invite God to join you in your practising of how "to be with God ?" Before you begin to meditate, ask God to hear you, to help you, and to instruct you on how to achieve this union.

Then there is all the rest of God's creation beyond us. Can we really feel comfortable in doing something all the time just for ourselves ? Is there not a point in our spiritual evolution when we need to wholeheartedly share any benefits we receive—when we have been given the grace to do something to further our connection with God ?

Tibetan Buddhist teachings first introduced me to the idea of sharing and including all sentient beings in prayer before I did any spiritual practice. I am grateful for this gift. How can we possibly try to do anything for ourselves when we are truly all one and united in our Divinity? If I am ever feeling upset by something someone has done or said or that life is unfair, I have been helped to rise above this by thinking something like:

How can I ever resent anyone, when we are all in this one big soup pot of life and suffering together? No one is exempt from suffering. No one will ever be in this pot of Maya alone. And no matter how good it looks for anyone, we are all suffering in the way that is most relevant to us. This soup pot has amazing properties. It knows exactly which ingredient will make you suffer the most and this will not necessarily make someone else suffer in the same way. But whatever ingredient you get will be just right for you.

As a result, I am happy to know and use this Tibetan Buddhist prayer :

By the power and the truth of this practice;
May all beings have happiness and the causes of happiness;
May all be free from sorrow and the causes of sorrow;
May all never be separated from the sacred happiness which is sorrowless;
And may all live in equanimity, without too much attachment and too much aversion,
And live believing in the equality of all that lives.

What to Meditate on

This may seem a contradictory thing to say, but what we meditate on with our minds is our mind itself. We do this by focusing on some object to engage the mind and actually to give the mind something to do. Remember, what is important is giving the mind something to focus on. But is the object that important?

I have to say that it is important to me what I meditate on, and I never could get used to the idea or enjoy meditating by focussing on the tip of my nose. But there are people I know who do this and who get very good results. After all, as we said earlier, it is concentration that is important in stopping the thoughts and allowing union with God to take place. If one concentrates, say, unwaveringly on the tip of one's nose, one allows the mind to become absorbed in a singular thought—here, in the thought of one's nose! This means one is experiencing single–pointed, pure contemplation which is one of the aims of meditation.

When you engage the mind in this exclusive way, you allow the mind to be so engaged that *you* can connect to God, which is of course the main purpose of the meditation.

The aim of concentration and meditation is to feel close to God. The aim is to feel no separation from God.

So, I would suggest that whether you wish to contemplate on the tip of the nose or anything else, that you wholeheartedly include God! That way, you acknowledge very consciously that you are Divine and, so therefore is your nose. You are contemplating a Divine nose and not just a nose. Then God is included in every way, not just in that space left when the mind is fully engaged in contemplation. But, your thoughts are focussed on God and not just your nose. I suggest that you do this in any form of meditation you practise, and in that way you will never get carried away with the mental acrobatics.

The following are some of the ways I have meditated by myself, or when facilitating a group of people, and which I have found to be helpful:

Focus on the spiritual centre of your heart. It is located on the right side of the Heart Chakra, while the physical heart is to the left. Place your consciousness there whilst you meditate or chant. Your heart centre is the seat of the Buddha Mind, the Wisdom Mind. Concentrate on it. Visualise the spiritual heart within the Heart Chakra. See a lotus with 12 open petals, which is symbolic of the Heart Chakra.

Tibetan Buddhist teachings speak of "Bringing the Mind Home." This is based on the ignorance of our true nature, which the

Buddha saw. In stripping the mind of this ignorance, the Buddha realised that suffering itself would end. Meditation for Buddhists is *to bring the mind home and to rid the mind of its ongoing habit of being distracted.*

The Ajna centre, or Third Eye, is also considered to be one of the powerful centres to mediate upon. This energy centre is situated between the eyebrows. Sai Baba refers to meditation and the Ajna centre saying:

When mind begins to wander hither and thither one must engage it. If mind does not have anything to do it would roam the whole world... So, before sitting for meditation, one must assign some work to the mind. What type of work? It has been a known fact that mind is a mad monkey. To make a monkey busy while he performs other feats, the street performer would plant a stick in the ground and ask the monkey to repeatedly go up and down the stick. Similarly we must assign the job of a watchman to the mind near that part of forehead where eyebrows join. By constant practice, we can make the mind stay in one place...

Many exponents of meditation and the Chakras say that the Ajna centre is the most appropriate for meditation, because of its potential to open the meditator up to Total Seeing. Paradoxically, in spite of this great potential, the Ajna also regulates and balances the other Chakras at the same time. You might think of the Ajna as a Master Chakra, and therefore it is considered one of the safest centres to focus on when meditating. So, when fully concentrating on the Third Eye, all the Chakras can be appropriately opened and purified in a balanced and healing way.

According to most Chakra Masters, if you meditate on the Ajna centre, you will eradicate all your sins and impurities, and you will be able to enter the next level of the 7th Chakra, the Crown Chakra, which is that of Realisation. This Chakra opening is known as the place where you can go beyond all the kinds of desires that motivate life and impel you to move in many directions. It helps to facilitate the one-pointedness you need in order to truly meditate.

In meditating, I have also found it helpful to concentrate on the Crown Chakra and visualising a lotus on the crown of my head, symbolising the thousand-petal lotus depicting this energy. The ultimate result of meditation on the Crown Chakra, and which an adept achieves, is immortality and Realisation — where there is no activity of the mind and no knower. There is no knowledge or anything to be known. Knowledge, the knower and the known all become unified and liberated. This is called *Samadhi* and is the pure bliss of total inactivity. Here, all feelings, emotions, and desires, which are the activities of the mind, are dissolved into their Source, God, and union is realised.

Here, one becomes *Sat-Chit-Ananda* (Being-Awareness-Bliss). One is one's own Real Self. As long as one stays in the physical body one retains non-dual consciousness, enjoying the *leela* (God's play) without becoming troubled by pleasure and pain, honours and humiliations.

People can often experience glimpses of these states but not stay permanently in them. I know of many people who have had such experiences and who can even become depressed when the experience leaves them, and they feel as though they have not achieved anything. I have also had some similar experiences, but rather than feel depressed about them I view them as glimpses of what is waiting for me when I truly come home to my Self. I trust the timing, for all timing is God's timing and therefore can never be wrong. There is a right time for everything and everyone !

It is like wanting to get inside the most beautiful house which I know is mine, but for the time being I am not able to. And so, I hang around the grounds, which are also beautiful, and I try to at least get some glimpses inside as I walk past the windows.

Then, one day, the front door opens and I am allowed a preview of what, at the right time, will be mine, and where I will be allowed to remain forever. And, it is so, so beautiful a vision that it fills my heart with such joy. Then the door is closed again. The vision is gone. But I know what is mine and where I will one day be living and no one and nothing can ever take that away from me.

The following is one such glimpse I had a few years ago. It was not a direct result of meditation, as I was not meditating at the time.

I was sleeping when it began, but it was a result of practises that I had been doing prior to the event, and I was consequently ripe for the experience. It was not long after my letter-writing experiences with Sai Baba in Kodaiknal and the interview with Him that followed. The moment fully uplifted me and now I know that one day, this realm of reality will be permanently mine:

Divine Comedy

I am dreaming that I am speaking to someone on the telephone. The voice is telling me that my mother has died. I am feeling shocked. Thoughts are buzzing in my head, and I feel the most tremendous grief. I am hearing a long, drawn-out internal scream which is saying, "Oh no, I shall never hear her voice again."

I am aware that I am in India and that my mother has died in Scotland. Our separation is final and there is no going back.

As I am feeling all of this I awake and I am sitting on my bed. It is the middle of the night. My husband is asleep beside me. But I am sitting up and my right arm and hand are raised as though I am holding a telephone. Everything feels very acute and sharp, heightened. Even so, my mind feels completely disoriented. I am confused as to whether I really dreamed this or not or whether it is true and that my mother has died. It feels as though she really has died.

At the same time, I realised that I was having a heart attack. The grief was too much and my heart was in spasm and I was feeling the most acute and sharp pain. The extreme hurting was travelling down my left arm. I was aware that I was dying and that there was absolutely nothing I could do about it. I could not speak or get my breath and I felt immobile. At that point, and like my earlier childhood drowning experience, I saw two separate scenes about three feet in front of me. They were like two cinema screens projected out into the dark space of the room in front of me.

My Guru, Sai Baba, was in each scene. But it was as though He was like the old-time comedians Laurel and Hardy, with a sprinkling of Charlie Chaplin. Both images of Sai Baba were communicating with one another from one screen to the other screen in a comical, slapstick way. And I could see one Sai Baba image twirling a stick in the way Charlie Chaplin had done. This last vision seemed to put the tin lid on the whole episode for me and, of course, I found nothing funny at all in the farce.

In fact, I felt devastated. Here I was dying with a heart attack. Presumably my mother had just died. While feeling the most grief I had ever experienced, I watched The One I looked to as God, The One I relied on in times of need, The One Whose Love and Compassion I believed in, doing a comical duo act right in front of my eyes. Oh God, I thought, I cannot bear it anymore. And internally I screamed at Him, "How could You—How could You be so callous? How could You be so cruel?"

In that instant, when I thought I could bear this farce no longer, my mind literally detonated. In retrospect, I suppose it was a bit like when a computer crashes. Suddenly, my mind and its thoughts, just like a computer when it crashes, stopped and there was nothing. No thoughts, no pain, no sense of me as I knew myself. There was no concern whether anyone was dying or had even been born. It was as though I had died and had suddenly awoken, and all that experience of that whole life had been a dream and was irrelevant. I was Being, Awareness and Bliss. There was no sense of where I began and ended. I was not the body. There was nothing to do and there was no thought. I cannot say "I" was aware. There was no "I". The closet expression of the truth would be that Consciousness was aware of Itself. I do not know how long I was like this. It could have been for a second or for an hour. There was no sense of time.

Then Consciousness observed thoughts coming back into my mind. They moved like little, marching soldier ants. I watched them as they came nearer and nearer, approaching from the sides of my eyes about to enter my body through my head. As they did so, my body began to feel itself again, and I was aware of "me" with senses, thoughts, and emotions. As the soldier-ant thoughts marched closer still, I felt some of the former pain returning, but it was not as severe. And then I was aware that there had been a contraction, that my mind had stopped, as I said, and that now my mind had begun again. This time it noted that I was not frightened. I was excited because I knew that I had undergone a profound mystical experience. But, nevertheless, I was still angry with my Guru for making a mockery or my suffering, my impending death, and for ignoring the fact that my mother had died in the dream.

It took me quite a while to integrate and understand the whole experience. I now know that the death I experienced was the death of *The Mother*, (the Archetype) not my actual mother, although she, of course, represented this symbol for me. The death of *The Mother* meant the death of everything that I had identified with as being able to hold me, contain me and to which I could cling to up to that point in my life. Once *The Mother* was dead, all the preconceptions I had held fell away. They had been lies. The mind thinks it knows what we need to cling to, what is fair, what it is protected by, but Sai Baba revealed in this example that my mind did not have a clue about the truth. In fact, when my mind was presented with the ultimate truth that nothing material exists, that the Absolute is Sat-Chit-Ananda, it could no longer function.

On the other hand, my body felt quite bruised, especially in the region of the heart, for some days following this event. When the initial excitement of my glimpse of Realisation faded, I still could not understand the full meaning of what had happened to me and why. But more awareness of the meaning followed in the months ahead.

Since then, I still have many moments of loss, grief, upset, trauma, and it is as though God has tested me even more than before. I do not want to bore you with the details of my losses because, in effect, the pain I suffer is no different than yours, but the miracle is that I am also able to laugh at it from time to time. In fact, I have peace regardless. This ability to laugh at my troubles and to have peace in spite of them has kept me sane.

However, on the surface I find myself reacting and going through the motions of grief, for example, as though it is expected. At the same time, I am aware of a *Deep Knowing* that I cannot take anything material or worldly that seriously anymore.

Sai Baba's comical antics in the face of my then grave feelings of enormous grief made me realise this. He proved to me that I am more than this body, the hurts, the feelings, the reactions and the blitz of thoughts. He showed me how, in the face of my True Reality (God), these things we feel to be so significant are not important, and they are even funny!

I understand now how Poonjaji could suddenly roar with laughter when listening to someone's narration of a supposedly serious situation and of what seemed to be his or her most important sufferings. He was not being callous or cruel. In the clarity of his knowledge of Truth these sufferings were hilarious. I used to watch him as he tried, impossibly, to keep a straight face, so as not to hurt the narrator of the tragedy. But then his eyes would glisten, his large tummy would shake, and his lips would tremble. All of a sudden there was no holding back the laughter. He would just roar!

I used to think that I understood what was happening, but really this was only from the narrowness of my mind's understanding. After the comedy cinema presentation by Sai Baba I really did know what this humour was all about. I am so grateful to have had a glimpse of my own Divinity and a peek through the doorway of my real abode. In my opinion, this is what meditation is for, to take us home.

Meditation

I remember asking Rinpoche in Sikkim about what the aim of all the spiritual practices was. It seemed to me, at the time, that there was a lot of trying, a lot of visualising, getting into postures and such effort involved. But then what? Rinpoche laughed and he told me a little tale :

The Tantric Key

A monk was very intent on his spiritual progress and so he made a tremendous effort each day for many hours to do his spiritual training and meditations. He did this for many years, but he did not seem to be getting anywhere. He thought perhaps that there was one more difficult practice that he needed to master and which his Guru had kept from him. Perhaps the Guru is keeping this secret until I am ready, the monk, thought.

Eventually, he got the courage to speak to his Guru and to ask him what to do next. He spoke of how he had practised all the meditations, tantras and rituals. He had suffered severe hardships and austerities but now he wanted the Big Prize. He wanted the magic, tantric key which would liberate him! The Guru listened patiently and finally relented and He gave His disciple the secret. Whispering in his ear, He told the monk to forget all his practices, everything that he had learned, and to, "Just relax."

Relaxation, Rinpoche explained to me, is one of the highest sadhanas (spiritual practises). One has to make a lot of effort before being able to be spiritually ripe enough to get the benefits of relaxing. And, this little story reveals one of the greatest secrets of meditation.

After all the concentration, the trying, the necessary effort, and when you finally reach the point where the thoughts cease, if only for a moment, you relax. You let go and you just exist.

At this point, to keep trying to do anything more would be an intrusion, a disruption of the natural peace present. Your meditation has been successful. It brought you to this point. Now you are here! Let go. Don't try. Just be. You have become That which you were seeking (God).

Here is another way of putting it:

It is as if you know that you want to go somewhere and you have to travel there by bus. So, you find out the route you need and you purchase your ticket. You make sure you are at the right bus stop, and then you get on the bus. The bus starts moving and you begin travelling toward your destination. Now, when you get to your stop, you ought to get off. It would be very silly to stay on the bus, wouldn't it? You would not reach your destination. If you stay on the bus, you will need to pay a further fare and you will end up somewhere you did not intend to go.

The practice of meditation is like that. It is only a practice, a journey to take you somewhere, and when you get to the right stop you need to get off and enjoy your destination. Do not go on the journey and forget to get off the bus. Do not forget what you started the journey for. You are using a means of transport to reach God, to go "home" to God. Do not get too attached to the vehicle, to the journey, or to the scenery along the way. You might forget your destination and forget to step off...

Some people get so attached to the techniques of meditation that they lose sight of their goal. And, sadly, many of them go mad in the process. There is a limit to everything, just as there is right timing for everything. See the chapter at the end of this section for advice on how to avoid the pitfalls of meditation practise.

In the beginning, it helps to have an experienced teacher or a tried and tested way. Otherwise you may find yourself on that bus for years, never reaching your destination, merely going around and around in circles.

So, what might you experience in meditation? People often do not know what meditation is, and so they do not know if they have truly experienced it or not. Some people tell me in workshops that they think that they have never experienced meditation because they have never been aware of their thoughts ceasing. This is enough to make them so despondent that they stop trying to meditate.

I have also heard some funny, true stories about people who sit 30 minutes a day and then think that they are Yogis. (A Yogi is adept at union with God.) For example, one professor, whilst smoking a cigarette with his left hand and holding a glass of red Bordeaux in his right, told the guests at his cocktail party that he was now a Yogi because he had completed his 1500 US dollars, three-week course in meditation. That was all there was to it he thought, and that he had passed the finals !

There is a humorous saying in the UK that represents the "New Age" and its sometimes quick fixes :

"I've been there, I've done it. I've got the tee-shirt to prove it!"

Anonymous

In *The Tibetan Book of the Living and Dying* there is a very clear explanation of meditation, where the mind is compared to a jar of muddy water.

The more we leave the water without interfering or stirring it, the more the particles of dirt will sink to the bottom, letting the natural clarity of the water shine through. The very nature of the mind is such that if you only leave it in its unaltered and natural state, it will find its true bliss and clarity.

In the experience of meditation, we just relax and ignore the thoughts. How I wondered, do we avoid stirring the muck? This is what I perceived:

Imagine that the particles of muck are your thoughts. They are in your mind just as dirty particles are in a pool or lake. Do not follow your thoughts. Do no stir them up. Now see your thoughts as you would see the dirt particles in the lake. Watch them arise and watch them fall. Do not let them expand. See them losing their weight and their momentum. Watch these thoughts as they sink to the bottom of your mind. Now behold the natural clarity of your mind.

Remember, though, that when you become more still the thoughts will not go away. In fact, they may even become more noticeable. In meditation, the thoughts are there. But you, with your power of concentration must not follow them.

If you do not follow them they are like seeds yet to sprout, and they may even disappear if you do not water them with your attention. So, there is no need to be frustrated or feel that you are a failure. As long as you have a mind, thoughts will come. Let them. Be allowing, be still, be relaxed and be at peace. Enjoy a communion with your True Self, with God.

After Meditation

In real Dhyana, (Meditation) you soon get over the consciousness that you are doing Dhyana. In fact, every moment of your life must be a moment utilised for Dhyana.

That is the best way to live. When you sweep your rooms tell yourself that your hearts too have to be swept likewise; when you cut vegetables feel that lust too has been cut into pieces. Desire, in addition, that your love may take in wider and wider circles and expand even into the regions of strangers and foes. This is the means by which you can make your home a hermitage and the routine of living into a route to Liberation.

Sri Sathya Sai Baba

In this split and dualistic world we are a part of, we need to amend the old habits of disunion, and get into the habit of integration instead. You enhance the split, if you meditate for 30 minutes in the morning, then hurriedly have breakfast, and quickly get ready for work. Next, you jump into the car and at the first set of traffic lights when another car suddenly pulls out in front of you, you scream, rant and rave at the driver.

Many of us continue in this vein throughout the day. We arrive home in the evening, exhausted and feeling fragmented and then we sit for another 30-minute meditation. What is it all about? Is there any point here in even trying to meditate?

It has been my experience in working with people that this kind of split can do us more harm than good. Often whatever benefits gained during meditations are lost as soon as the so-called meditator encounters confrontation, harassment and frustration. The shift from peace to disharmony is so sharp that it causes the split.

In the above example, the 30-minute meditation in the morning may have helped to bring that person into a more realistic, sensitive place in connection with himself. However, if he then carelessly ignores his openness and enters the world so exposed, it is like smashing himself on the head with a hammer. A daily repetition of this can hardly be good for the nervous system.

When one is initially so stressed and split, it would be better to just try and relax one's breathing throughout the day. This is another form of meditation. Or perhaps, do not do the meditation in the morning, but do it before going to bed at night.

I have personally seen spectacular results when people have attempted to follow their breathing throughout the day, rather than splitting time off from their daily lives "to do meditation." If one is aware of one's breathing, as much as possible, one can recognise when it is slow, fast, stopped, laboured and when it feels good. This can help someone to know what is happening to him or to her emotionally. In helping the breathing to be more normal and peaceful, you can feel the benefit. This regulation of the breathing balances the entire body, mind and emotions. You feel more at ease, at peace and in harmony. (See next chapter for more on breathing.)

The quote at the beginning of this section tells us how to integrate meditation into our lives. What's more, we can use our increasing concentration and awareness of the true nature of the mind to find God in everything we do and in everything we see and in everyone we speak to. Our moments of concentrated meditation, when we sit for periods of time, are then a *practice* to help us use in our daily lives the truth we find. In this way we unify the split which has separated us from God, our True Nature and our True Reality.

Just as in the beginning of meditation, at the end we can include all sentient beings to share in our meditation; we can also share any benefits from the results we may have gained spiritually from any practice we do. There are formal Buddhist prayers for this conclusion, but one's own heartfelt words can suffice as a final dedication prayer. One can say something like this:

Dear God,
May You take all that I have spiritually gained
in the doing of this practice
to share it equally with all beings.
May You take all the peace and joy I have received
from You to share it equally with all beings.
May you take all my merit gained
in the doing of this and other practices
to be used for the benefit and enlightenment of all beings.
In deepest gratitude,
Mynavati

Preliminaries to Specific Meditations and Visualisations

9

No one can train another person in meditation.
It is possible to teach pose,
posture and breathing.
But meditation is a function of the inner man.
It involves deep subjective quiet, the emptying of the mind
and the filling of oneself with the light that emerges from
the Divine Spark within.
No textbook or teacher can teach this.

Sri Sathya Sai Baba

Before we begin to do any of the techniques outlined in this chapter, it is helpful to look at the conditions that ease our ability to meditate. Adepts can meditate anywhere. I once saw a painting of a Buddha sitting in meditative posture in the middle of a New York shopping mall. His face was serene and calm and he was completely unperturbed by the activity, noise and hustle bustle all around him. This image and its implications struck me, and it is one I have never forgotten. This is our aim in meditating, to be able to be anywhere and in any conditions and still be able to be at one with our Divine Self, with God. But, most of us need to develop this ability first. So, it makes sense to help ourselves in every way possible.

Appropriate Conditions for Meditation Practice

1. Choose any quiet place where you can be alone and where you can feel comfortable. This is important because not every part of a room or corner of a room is personally comfortable to us.

For praying and meditating many people choose a place to sit facing East. This has been a direction noted as being used for spiritual practices for as long as man has recorded his devotional activities. The sun rises in the East, and it has been symbolically related to God for centuries. For example, if we sit facing the East towards the rising sun, we are receptive to the Light of the Divinity rising within. The image of the rising sun is especially evocative if we meditate at dawn.

2. Attempt to be purposeful, focused, and vigilant, but try also not to be anxious about the results. If you worry about results rather than just allowing yourself to be, you might focus on what is going to happen, and worse, what might *not* happen. As a result, you could end up being more agitated than before attempting the meditation, and the experience you wished to achieve would definitely not occur. It would have been better for you to sit down on a comfortable chair, have a cup of tea or coffee, and watch television !

Many people today, especially in the West, are super-achievers. They have become bound up in the result of things relative to what they think is expected. They give themselves extra pressure, as if they do not have enough already. They take their worldly ambitions of trying to gain a promotion, a pay raise and praise from their superiors and drag them into their little spiritual corners of supposed tranquillity. Chogyam Trungpa Rinpoche, one of the first Gurus to bring Tibetan Buddhist teachings to America, called these people, "spiritual materialists."

As Trungpa pointed out, the spiritual path requires giving up rather than increasing our attachment for achievement and praise. In his book *Cutting Through Spiritual Materialism,* Trungpa advocated that some kind of sacrifice is needed and that we must give up our ambition to get something in return for our gift.

So the point we come back to is that some kind of real gift or sacrifice is needed if we are to open ourselves completely. This gift may take any form. But in order for it to be meaningful, it must entail giving up our hope of getting something in return. It does not matter how many titles we have, not how many suits of exotic clothes we have worn through, not how many philosophies, commitments and sacramental ceremonies we have participated in. We must give up our ambition to get something in return for our gift. That is the really hard way.

Chogyam Trungpa

So, for success in meditating you have to let go of all ideas of achieving anything. If you can do this, and just allow yourself to be open and receptive, you may get a wonderful surprise! At the very least, you will lessen the chance of remaining self-centred and motivated by small-minded thoughts.

3. Remember that you are Divine and that in your meditation you are opening up to all that is Divine and Infinite. As we say, it is easy to forget this when we get caught up in the mind games of how to do a technique! Include God always. Invite God in the beginning, in the middle and at the end. And then when you leave your meditative sitting posture to go out into the world or to do any other activity that is supposedly not meditation, take God with you. Ask God to accompany you, and your meditation can go on and on in the most exquisite way.

4. Do not let your mind attempt to analyse or understand too much, before, during and after your meditation. Once the mind tries to understand anything spiritual, it immediately limits and places its confines or its own ignorance on the happening. How can the mind understand God? The mind will never understand the expansiveness or totality of God. In this way, the mind can never really understand meditation. That is why we have to give the mind something to engage it, like focussing on an object, while we do the meditation. It is that simple. So, never trust the mind and its multitude of thought servants. It will only limit you, confuse you and turn the potentially Divine and fabulous into the ordinary and mundane. In this way, you will also not get caught up in judgements and comparisons.

5. Try not to get too caught up in the experiences. This means either the good or the bad experiences. They are both merely experiences after all. What people usually do with experiences is identify wholeheartedly with them and use them as a gauge of how successful they are in their undertakings. But good experiences can make you pompous and arrogant and full of pride (which is the last thing you are meant to be feeling on the spiritual path). And, what we consider to be bad experiences, like "nothing is happening" could make you feel hopeless, despondent and ready to give up.

Experiences are not the Ultimate Reality. They are precursors, happenings that suggest what can come, but they are not the real thing. It is always important to remember this. Never lose sight of the goal you are seeking. The goal you are seeking is to unite with God. Trust that whatever is happening to you is absolutely appropriate for you and, again, do not judge or make comparisons. How can you understand what God is doing for you and why? God knows best, and God is preparing you always to know your own Divinity. Often, when we think that nothing is happening, God is doing even more for us than we can possibly imagine.

Other Practical and Sensible Considerations for Meditation Practice

Sit for periods of 2 minutes and 24 seconds
or
a *maximum* of 20-30 minutes twice a day.
or
within that allotted time,

Sit until you feel you are getting dozy
or
that you have had enough.
Trust your own wisdom
and
respect your capabilities and limitations.
You have them for a reason.
The length of time that you sit is not so important
as
the quality of the time you sit for meditation.
Do not over stretch yourself.
Remember that you are not in a race, or a marathon,
and there is no finishing flag to your
Spiritual development.
A useful time to meditate is in the early
morning and early evening hours.
Why ?

One reason is that in the early morning,
the time of the day is peaceful and quiet
and
the busy activities of the day have not yet begun.
In the evening, the time of the day
becomes peaceful and quiet again
and
the daily tasks have been completed.
The mind can find peace in this awareness that it has *time.*
Also,
in the morning, after waking, thoughts and feelings are still sleepy and inactive
and
it is easier to focus then on meditation.
In the evening,
when work is finished and the day is coming to an end,
meditation helps reduce stress and clears the mind and Consciousness
for sleep.

Importantly,
the **times** of the **day** have qualities
which make them more conducive to certain activities.

Sai Baba explains:

Time has three qualities:
Balanced, equal-minded (sathwa),
over-active, passionate (rajas)
and
dull, inactive (thamas).

At night-time, 8 p.m. to 4 a.m.
is considered our thamasic time.
During this period, even animals and birds sleep.

From 8 a.m. to 4 p.m.
is considered rajasic time.

Everyone is active with their daily duties during this period.

From 4 a.m. to 8 a.m.
is considered satwic time.
You should awaken by this time in the morning
and undertake your spiritual discipline and start your studies.
During the hours of 4 a.m. to 8 a.m.
the senses will be quiet.
There is no need to take a bath and
stimulate the senses.

It is easy to concentrate during that peaceful time.
Don't hesitate to wake up at 4 a.m.
Get up at 4 a.m., wash your face
to avoid sleepiness and sit for meditation.

If you observe these disciplines, meditation will become very easy.
In the evening also, after you finish your classes and games at school,
around 6 p.m., wash your face
and sit for meditation for at least 5 minutes.

You need only 2 minutes and 24 seconds for meditation, not hours.
Practice concentration and meditation and experience the results.
Your joy, purity, and brightness will be enhanced beyond measure.

A Daily Meditation Routine
will anchor you in life's ups and downs
and help keep you
centered on your Divinity and God.

Daily meditation practise will enhance your powers
of concentration.
And this, in turn,
will strengthen your ability
to divert your mind from its habitual attractions.
It is preferable and wiser to meditate on an empty to light stomach.

Your Body During Meditation

Breathing

Often, when we try to do something, our breathing immediately responds to our resultant feelings. If we observe this process, we can be aware that our breathing becomes fast, slow, irregular or sometimes we even stop breathing altogether for periods of seconds and then start again. If we take control of our breath by regulating it, we help our bodies and our whole beings to let go and relax for the process of the meditation.

As long as we are identified with our emotions and feelings, our breath will be subject to irregularity. If we can at least be aware of our breathing and help it to become calm and peaceful, natural and regular, we also help the emotions and feelings to calm. This is important in our meditation because at times our thoughts can become rampant in the initial stillness of the body and the space they find. In regulating our breathing, these thoughts and their emotional children can be pacified.

As well as this, in the East, breath control is seen as a way of enhancing the vital force of one's being and it is used as a meditation in itself. Regulating the inhaling and the exhaling of breath and the holding of the breath is called *Pranayama*. The Sanskrit word *Prana* means *vital force* or *cosmic energy*. It also signifies *life* or *breath*. *Ayama* means the control of *Prana*. Therefore, *Pranayama* means the control of the vital force by the concentration and regulation of our breathing. With controlled yogic breathing, we are able to enhance our vital force by refueling it. It is not difficult to see here the implications of the breath and how it effects us in body, mind and emotions.

You only need to observe your breathing when you are feeling low or upset and you will notice that it is irregular and slow. When angry, your breathing will become rapid and agitated. Your entire body, nervous system and endocrine glands will feel the effects of this disharmony. Like a never-ending circle, dysfunction on any level of your physiological body will effect your emotional body and the feelings that arise will be a direct result. These will disturb your capacity to meditate. In this way, one can see how everything begins and ends with the breath.

The subject of *Pranayama* is vast. There are many good books available on *Pranayama*. However, with such a technique, no book can compensate for the teaching from one who is a Master. There are many Yoga teachers and Masters who practise this art of breathing, and if you wish to explore the subject further seek those you feel are accomplished and caring and learn directly from them. Meanwhile, remember the power and the importance of regular breathing in your meditation.

Finally, Swami says, about breathing:

The 21,600 breaths per day is the typical experience. It is the average of one's life. At times of exertion or stress the breathing will be very fast; at times of peace and quiet it will be slow. Some people may have an average of more than 21,600 breaths per day. A practised yogi may average not 15 breaths per minute but as low as 6 or 7 per minute. The slower the breathing the longer the life span.

The short-life monkey will breathe some 40 times per minute. The long-life snake will breathe 3 or 4 times per minute.

Posture

I came to meditation relatively late in years. By that time, I was used to slumping about in cosy easy chairs. My back and spine were already worn out because I was a nurse during my early twenties. Often, I had to lift heavy patients. What's worse, I did this lifting in the wrong way. Later, I worked in an office sitting in the wrong posture at a desk, bending over papers day in and day out.

Gradually, my work conditions improved when I became a psychic and healer at The Edinburgh College of Parapsychology and a psychotherapist in private practice. But I was still doing a lot of sitting in inappropriate chairs. I spent my time leading groups and workshops. I conducted the groups and gave sessions on fairly good, upright, but comfortable chairs with the luxury of a back cushion if needed. If only I had realised at the time just how much of a luxury this all was.

When I came to India, my body received the biggest shock that could ever have happened to it. I had to adjust to Indian-style beds. This was either a mat on the floor or a thin, hard mattress on a wooden board. And, there was no bath to soak in, to help my battered and bruised back that had been used to the best kind of mattress and the softest feather pillows. If I wanted to have *Satsang* (good company of like-minded spiritual seekers) or teachings I had to sit for hours on a hard floor with my legs crossed.

Of course, I could not sit like this for very long and suffered pain in my back and legs. I fidgeted constantly and when I tried to uncross my legs and give them some relief I had to find a way of placing them where my feet did not point towards the Guru in front of me as this was considered disrespectful. There were always people sitting to either side of me, and so I would have to do some, previously unknown-to-me, contortions to find an opening to place my, by now, agonisingly painful legs, ankles and feet.

Experiencing all this discomfort there was no way I could enter any kind of meditation. My whole being was intent on what seemed to be physical survival and relief from pain. Eventually, my left leg "dropped" and I was able to let it rest on the ground in a crossed legged-position, but my right leg has only been able to do this partially to this day. For me, The Lotus Position is still out of reach. Yet, I meditate and pray and now I can manage this without having to think too much about my body.

So, do not be discouraged if you feel that your body cannot sit in the way some books tell you. If you can, for example, sit in the Lotus Position, this is wonderful and I congratulate you. You are indeed fortunate. But if you cannot do this, it is not a disaster and it need not necessarily hinder you.

In meditating and in praying it is helpful to sit on the floor, but one can prop oneself up with cushions, or lean against a wall and this can help to make you quite comfortable. Why sit on the ground? The ground, the floor, has a magnetic *earthing* effect, and this helps you to go into an inner, quieter space. Also, it is important that the spine is straight, for different reasons, when you do any kind of spiritual practices. To maintain the correct posture for meditating it is easier to sit on the ground. If you have difficulty you can obtain meditation stools and flat, folding chairs which support the back.

Keep the spine straight when sitting for meditation because:

a) It will keep you more alert
and
b) energy passes through the spine via the Chakras when you meditate, and if your spine is bent or slumped, this energy can become trapped and cause physical, mental and emotional problems for you.

Sri Sathya Sai Baba says :

The spinal column should not bend to any side. Some people bend the neck and sit. This is very dangerous. If Kundalini power (the basic energy, creative force, lying dormant in the Root Chakra – Muladhara) were to get locked there, where many nerves are present, it would damage the person and cause paralysis. There are men who have damaged their heads/senses by wrongly adhering to Kundalini. One should not bend backwards. One should be so straight that if a nail were to be driven down from Sahasrara, (The Crown Chakra) it should appear as though the whole body were wrapped around the nail. Not only that, one should loosen the garment that is around the waist, it might, to an extent obstruct the Kundalini. Usually people who practice Kundalini Yoga are single garmented. So, waist should not be tightly bound. Vision should be centred at the tip of the nose. If one were to sit for meditation with open eyes, all those who pass by would cause disturbance to the mind. If the eyes are totally closed, the Goddess of sleep would envelop us. Therefore, we should have half-closed eyes posture. Some believe the tip of the nose to be between the eyebrows. No, it is forehead; it is the end of the nose i.e., tip of the nose that has to be concentrated on.

When we sit for meditation our body should not be in contact with anyone else's body. When one works with electricity, one would don some sort of insulation (wood/cloth) to insure against shock. Similarly, meditation also is a kind of power. It also would give a shock if two bodies touch. In every body there is current. The current goes/gets lost through nails, hair, eyes and speech. In the olden days people allowed nails and hair to grow because they did not want the current to be wasted. It is due to that current that hair and nails grow and eyes and other organs function…

In *The Tibetan Book of Living and Dying*, posture is explained as:

Sit, then, as if you were a mountain, with all the unshakeable, steadfast majesty of a mountain. A mountain is completely natural and at ease with itself, however strong the winds that batter it, however thick the dark clouds that swirl around its peak. Sitting like a mountain let your mind rise and fly and soar.

The most essential point of this posture is to keep the back straight, like "an arrow" or "a pile of golden coins." The "inner energy" or "Prana" will then flow easily through the subtle channels of the body, and your mind will find its true state of rest. Don't force anything. The lower part of the spine has a natural curve; it should be relaxed but upright. Your head should be balanced comfortably on your neck. It is your shoulders and the upper part of your torso that carry the strength and grace of the posture, and they should be held in strong poise, but without any tension.

Sit with your legs crossed. You do not have to be in the full- lotus position, which is emphasised more in advanced yoga practice. The crossed legs express the unity of life and death, good and bad, skilful means and wisdom, masculine and feminine principles, samsara and nirvana; the humor of non-duality. You may also choose to sit on a chair, with your legs relaxed, but be sure always to keep your back straight.

Eyes Open or Closed

Most meditation masters suggest that you keep your eyes open during meditation. usually in a half-closed eyes position. In this way you are less likely to feel sleepy. When concentrating with one's eyes open, one focuses on an external object, but with one's eyes half closed, on what does one focus? As Sai Baba says above, one can focus on the tip of one's nose.

As well as this, one need not focus on anything in particular, but instead:

> *Turn back into yourself slightly, and let your gaze expand and become more and more spacious and pervasive.*
>
> *The Tibetan Book of Living and Dying*

And so, with the considerations of posture, breath and eyes let us look at a few examples of specific meditations I am familiar with, practice myself and which people I have worked with find helpful.

The Jyothi Meditation

10

The Jyothi (Light) meditation is one of the oldest recorded meditations in the Scriptures of India. Sai Baba has told us it is one of the safest. He tells us to do this meditation every day, without a break, for as long as we enjoy it and we will be purified and with God.

I usually lead people into this meditation when I facilitate a healing or meditation group and the feedback I receive is always heartening. The meditation is accessible to anyone who wants to try it and before long it can be mastered. I know many people now who use it in their daily offering of themselves to God.

I stay with the main theme of the original meditation but have found myself, over the years, using more modern words and sometimes, when seemingly appropriate, the meditation is slightly expanded in the concepts and this has been fitting for a particular group.

The meditation begins by asking the meditator to gaze at a flame from a candle or a lamp. A flame never diminishes its radiance no matter how many other candles or lamps are lit from it. In this way it symbolises the Absolute. Of course, this is the preferred option but a flame is not always convenient for people. In such a case I have advised people to *imagine* a flame in front of them.

Begin by sitting comfortably, with your back straight, in front of the flame or imaginary flame.

Imagine a flame before you.
Look deeply into this flame where you can see
its brightest, purest, white light.
Close your eyes
and from the Ajna centre,
the centre between your eyebrows,
allow the flame to enter you.
Allow the light to enter you,
and illuminate your entire being.

The light fills you and shines
into the lotus of your heart.

The lotus of your heart waits patiently for the light.
As the light shines on the lotus of your heart,
The petals open, one by one.
One petal, two petals, three petals opening to the light.
Four petals five petals, six petals uncurling,
seven petals, eight petals, nine petals, opening wider still,
10 petals, 11 petals, 12 petals,
unfolding to the light
to the warmth,
the love of this radiant light.

Let the light flow and expand from the lotus of your heart
entering your arms.
Feel this light illuminate and pulse
through each cell of your arms and hands,
physical and subtle,
to your very fingertips.
With this light in your arms,
your arms can only be used for goodness.
With this light in your arms and hands,
you help and soothe all those who come before you.
With this light in your arms and hands,
you can only give and receive in Truth and goodness.

Let this light expand from the lotus of your heart
and flow into your legs and feet.
Feel this light illuminate and pulse through
each cell of your arms and feet,
to the tips of your toes,
physical and subtle.
With this light in your
legs and feet
you can only stand in goodness.

With this light
in your legs and feet
you can only walk in Truth.
With this light in your legs and feet
you can only be where you are meant to be.

Let this light expand
from the lotus of your heart
and enter your tongue.
Let this light illuminate every particle of your tongue,
physical and subtle.
With this light in your tongue,
you can only taste that which is sweetness and goodness.
With this light in your tongue,
you can only speak that which is Truth.
With this light in your tongue,
your voice is a soothing balm.

Let this light expand
from the lotus of your heart
and enter your eyes.
Let this light illuminate your eyes entirely,
physical and subtle.
With this light in your eyes,
you can only see that which is goodness.
With this light in your eyes,
you can see the beauty and the harmony
in all creation.
With this light in your eyes,
you can see the Divine play of God
in all things.

Let this light expand
from the lotus of your heart
and enter your ears.
Let this light fill every cell of your ears,

physical and subtle.
With this light in your ears,
you can only hear the Truth and that which is goodness.
With this light in your ears,
you can hear the Divine sound
and the harmony in all of God's creation.

Let this light expand and flow
from the lotus of your heart
to your entire head,
physical and subtle.
With this light in you head,
your thoughts can only be those of goodness.
With this light in your head,
your mind is calm and at peace.
With this light in your head,
your mind is at one with God and all living things.

Let the light expand
from the lotus of your heart
to everyone and everything around you.
Let the love flow from your heart
to every corner of the room,
to every being, animate and inanimate.
Let the light flow.

Let the light expand
and flow from the lotus of your heart
to the entire place where you find yourself,
to the building
and to the streets beyond.
Let the light and the love
flow to everything and everyone,
in the villages, the cities, the towns,
the countries, the world.

Let this light flow
from the lotus of your heart
to all those whom you know and love,
to those who have helped you and cared for you.
Without them,
you would not be where you are now.
Let this light flow
in deepest loving gratitude
from the lotus of your heart.

Let this light expand further still and flow
from the lotus of your heart
to all those who have caused you pain,
to all those who have hurt you and harmed you.
Without them,
you would not be where you are now.
Let this light flow
in deepest loving gratitude
from the lotus of your heart.

Let this light expand further still and flow
from the lotus of your heart
to all those who are now being born
and to those who are taking their last breath.

Let this light flow
to all who are sick and in need of help
and to all those who are happy and in health.
Let this light flow to all those you know
and those you will never meet,
to every human being, animal, insect,
blade of grass and speck of dust,
to the entire creation of our Mother Earth.

Let this light expand further still and flow
from the lotus of your heart,

to the skies and the Universes beyond.
Visualise yourself holding
Creation between your loving hands.

Rest in the stillness.
Know that you are God.
Know that you are Divine.
Know that you are Light.
Know that you are Love.

Compassion
and
The Meditation of Giving and Receiving

11

The Meditation of Giving and Receiving, detailed here, is based on the Tibetan Buddhist *Tonglen* meditation. *Tonglen* in Tibetan means "giving and receiving." It is a way of meditation that powerfully invokes compassion within you. I was introduced to it in Sikkim when I first came to India and received instructions on meditation and Tibetan Buddhist practices and philosophy. Later, in my healing work with people who were not Buddhists and who were unfamiliar with Tibetan Buddhist terms and language I composed variations on the theme so that they could readily understand it. The examples I give here are from these variations.

The background and instruction to the formal Tibetan Buddhist practice of *Tonglen* can be found in many Tibetan Buddhist books, most notably, *The Tibetan Book of Living and Dying*. This book has a wealth of information on Buddhist philosophy and practices and a long section on the history and ways of practising *Tonglen*.

Shortly after my introduction to *Tonglen* and using the method, I had an experience that tested and evoked my compassion. This episode is proof of the power of compassion and how this Love can dissolve even the most terrifying fear from our hearts.

Letting Go of Fear

I was staying in Rinpoche's house in Sikkim where he and his family, his mother, father and siblings lived. Nearby there was a small and beautiful temple and one day I decided to visit it. When I did so, it was very quiet and no one else was around. I prostrated before the altar and sat for a short while in meditation. I liked being there very much.

I then returned back to my room in the house after going for a short walk. When I arrived back in my room I found that my door was open and my books and papers and mallas were in disarray. Some were on the floor and they were scattered. It looked as though children might have come into the room and thrown my belongings around. I did notice, however, that it was only my spiritual items and not my clothes that had been tampered with. I wondered if some of Rinpoche's nieces and nephews had visited and had done this. This seemed unlikely as they had never done this before and when they did visit they were always chaperoned. But I did not know how it possibly could have happened otherwise. I did not say anything. I thought it better not to. I tidied up and forgot about the incident.

During the night, however, I awoke with a feeling of someone being in my room. I was aware of the wind also. In Sikkim it is quite cold at night and fans are not necessary. But this was very intense wind, blowing into my face and I sat up in fear, not quite knowing what was happening. Suddenly my fear increased when I saw a large being standing in the doorway looking at me. The wind seemed to be coming from him. He resembled a man as well as a beast. And the wind was also swirling all around him, not just emanating from him. I was aware that some of my things were being scattered again. I leaned back against the wall, to the side of my bed and I felt as if my body was being pressed against the wall by the force of the wind. The skin on my cheeks and face was rippling as it was being pushed behind the bones in my skull

Suddenly he disappeared. I was terrified and I could not sleep the rest of the night. I did not know what this could mean or who he was. I was even frightened of telling Rinpoche, in case he thought I had gone mad. Who would believe me, I thought.

In the morning I found the courage to tell Rinpoche at breakfast what had happened. I expected him to totally disbelieve me or think that I was a lunatic. I also told him how I had found my belongings scattered when I had returned from the temple the day before. On hearing this, his eyes lit up as he realised that he had solved the mystery and he smiled saying, "Oh, I know who this is."

He explained that the Protector of the Temple, was most probably a Wind Being, who had been "captured" by the monks from one of the mountains a long time ago to guard the Temple. This explanation seemed as spectacular and astounding as my experience, but I, of course, believed Rinpoche and it made sense. Most likely this being had never seen anyone quite like me before, and so he had followed me. Yet, I was not relieved to know who the Wind Being was. In fact I got more scared. The idea of this Wind Being, this Protector of the Temple, having so much interest in me terrified me and I did not feel safe.

Around the same time that I had this experience I had been introduced to Tonglen, and I had been attempting to practice it. When I spoke of my intense fear about this Wind Being visiting me again, Rinpoche talked to me a little about it and of how, in fact, I should feel compassion for him, rather than fear. I remember thinking, How can he possibly be asking me to have and feel compassion for this being when I am the victim? Such was my ignorance! Such was my self-seeking and self-grasping.

But that night, I was able to experience what Rinpoche meant. I felt frightened to relax or sleep ever again, but the tiredness took over and at some point during the night I found myself being aware that I was sleeping. What I experienced could be called a dream, however I was "awake" in the dream and so was aware of everything very lucidly as it happened. The Wind Being appeared. Like the night before, I saw him clearly. He looked like I imagined the legendary Yeti to look. He stood in my doorway, as he had done the night before, but unlike the previous night, I was aware that as I was sleeping and "dreaming" that this was most probably happening on a more subtle plane and not happening on the physical plane at the same time.

I felt terror as I looked at him standing in the doorway. I felt that he could do anything to me and that I would be helpless. The fact that I was experiencing this on a subtle level was, I felt, more frightening to me than when it had happened to me on the physical level. I suppose I was more frightened because I felt that there was no inner safe space, nowhere to hide, even in sleep. But I continued to feel the terror because he kept staring at me intensely.

Miraculously, I suddenly became aware of Rinpoche's words to me the day before, about my feeling compassion for this being. I was aware of Rinpoche as I heard the words, aware of seeing him inside my mind and feeling as though he was present. At this point, I unexpectedly and involuntarily felt compassion for this being standing in front of me. I felt so moved by his predicament, his ignorance, which mirrored my own ignorance, that my heart just opened in compassionate love for him, and all the fear I felt vanished.

I remember his round, questioning and confused eyes as he looked at mine. The rest of him seemed somewhat of a hairy blur. Nevertheless, I knew that the Wind Being could see the Divine love I felt for him emanating from my own eyes. This love then reflected back to me as he just softened and slowly dissolved into what I can only express as a mist of love. Everything became silent and still. There was no need to fear. Fear cannot survive in the embrace of True Love.

I never saw the Wind Being again. Yet, he taught me such a great lesson! I am still grateful to him for showing me how my heart needed to open. I pray that he too shared completely in the benefits from any grace and awareness I received that night.

It is experiences and times like these that I am shown, without any shadow of a doubt, how God is with us in every moment and happening of our lives. God patiently waits for the ripening of our buds of potential love to teach us at the most Divinely fitting times, what we need to understand in order to erase a little bit more of our ignorance. When I reflect on this very idea, I am filled with awe at the limitless Love, Compassion, Right Timing and Patience of God, for each and every one. In this way, God showed me the miracle of love through the Tonglen Meditation of Giving and Receiving.

A Variation of the Tibetan Tonglen Meditation for the Opening up to Love

Firstly, connect with a fear in you that you believe is holding you back from opening your heart further to its Truth of compassion and oneness in Love with God. This may be a fear of death, of being open, of being hurt, of even Love itself. Identify what it is for you and then practice the meditation.

One can do this meditation for anyone or anything, for world peace, for someone who is dying and also for your instances of hurt. You only need substitute the *object/concern* of the meditation. Here I will use an example of something many of us have a fear of and which separates us from God and all creation: *Opening to love.*

To begin,
relax your body and mind and breathing.
Bring to your awareness the knowing
that all things of this world are illusory and temporary.
Bring to your awareness the knowing
that you and all beings are veiled
in ignorance and suffering.
And in this knowing
feel as much compassion as you can,
for each and every one.

Let your mind, your thoughts,
rest in their true home.
Let them rest in your heart.

Ask God to be with you
and
to stand beside you
and
to support you throughout
this meditation.

Imagine in front of you
this fear of love itself.
This may be a person, who symbolises this for you,
or it can be an object,
for example,
a hardened and closed shrivelled heart.

Imagine that this image
holds and grasps to itself

every possible aspect of your fear.
Take your time and let this unfold
and reveal itself to you,
as you may not even be aware
of what this as yet entails.

Imagine this fear of love
and all that it embodies
form into a great swirling mass
of thick, dense, hot, dirty, black smoke.
And,
as you breathe in,
envision your Divine Heart
embracing
and welcoming
and drawing to itself
this mass entity of filth and negativity.
Know, as you do this,
that at the same time
all the self-grasping thoughts
of your own heart
are destroyed by this very action.

As you breathe out,
visualise that you are sending out
luminous, cool, brilliant, white light
to the hardened and shrivelled closed heart
which is afraid to open,
and which is only concerned with its own self.
Know that the light from your heart
is dissolving the heart's pain and fear.
Know without any doubt
that this hard and closed heart
now softens and opens
in trembling Awareness
of Compassionate Love.

Nothing can harm or destroy
the Divinity
of your own True Heart,
a heart which has limitless Compassion,
Love and Purity.
Know that every thing and every one
including you,
can be transformed
in the presence
of its Divine Love.

Repeat
by
breathing in
and
breathing out
in the same way
for
around 10 to 15 minutes.
Then
rest in the
silence
of your Heart Divine.

The So Ham Meditation
and
Reciting the Name of God

12

The following two meditations are ones you can do anywhere and at anytime. They connect you to God in the most immediate and intimate way. I have practised them whenever I feel the need to, when I have felt at risk, when I have felt vulnerable or overwhelmed or when I just want to feel close to God.

They can be done at a bus stop, during a tea break at work, or while shopping. I have even found myself doing them sometimes when I am talking to someone. They became so much a part of my life that even when I myself was not consciously trying to do one or the other, they just happened anyway, and while they did I could still pay full attention to the person talking to me. I also find either of them a soothing meditation to do as I go to sleep at night. Often, I like to visualise placing my head on the feet of God as I go to sleep, and as I do this I like to internally chant and breathe, *So Ham.*

Interestingly, when I needed to move from one apartment to another last year, where did I find myself a suitable residence? My address is Soham 1!

So Ham Meditation

To begin,
relax your body and mind and breathing.
Then with concentration on the breath,
breathe in "So."
As you breathe in "So" be aware
of breathing God into your entire being.
Imagine God, if you can, as pure, white, luminous Light
entering your every cell.
As you breathe out "Ham" be aware
of breathing out "you," as Divine pure Light.

So-Ham, (God and I),
So- Ham, (God and I),
So-Ham,
God and I are One.

Getting into the habit of uniting with God in this simple way takes no great effort. You will find that as you breathe, you are automatically saying *So Ham, So Ham, So Ham.* The closeness and unity with God is felt in the natural rhythm of breathing. In time, the *So Ham* sound merges with the breath in such a way that one hears Aum, the primordial sound of the Universe.

I have advised people who feel split from their spiritual selves, who feel distant from God and who say to me, "Yes, I would like to meditate, but I really do not have the time..." to do this practise. Even a few minutes every hour can have a dramatic effect. This is a perfect meditational practice for people who are in business, or people who have trauma to deal with, and who are under tremendous worldly, or emotional strains, who have deadlines and who have *no time.* In the cases where I have told people how to do this meditation and how to even practice it a few minutes every few hours, they have come back to me to tell me of their experiences of greater peace, equal mindedness, mental sharpness, and physical stamina. Some have told me how these few minutes a day have made them realise how much God is with them and how near.

Sri Sathya Sai Baba also instructs people how to meditate on *So Ham* using the breath and the opening and closing of the nostrils. He says:

The mind must be allotted some heavy piece of work to hold it down.
This work is called Dhyana (Meditation).
Keep the mind above the upper lip, between the two nostrils,
right in front of the bridge of the nose.
Inhale through the left nostril closing the right with the right thumb.
As the breath goes in, it utters So (meaning, He);
then exhale through the right nostril,
closing the left nostril with right thumb.

As the breath goes out, it utters Ham (meaning, I).
Inhale and exhale slowly and deliberately,
conscious of the identity of He (the Lord) and I (yourself)
which it asserts, until the
breathing and the awareness grow into an
unnoticed process.

Keep the mind as a watchman,
to note the incoming and outgoing breaths,
to listen with the inner ear to the
So Ham that the breath whispers,
and to witness the assertion of you being the Divine,
which is the core of the Universe.
This is the Dhyana that will give victory.

Make So Ham the japam
(repetition of the Name or sacred mantra)
of the mind and you will be saved.
"I" will merge in the Universal.

Namasmarana
Repetition of the Name of God

This age that we are in right now is described by many Scriptures as the Kali Yuga (The age of Kali, Goddess of Destruction). This is a cyclical age that is considered to be the darkest time in the never-ending cycles of creation. It is written that during this Yuga, there is no human being on the planet without some darkness in his or her heart. Because it is such a dark time in human beings' spiritual lives it does not take great spiritual disciplines or meditational feats to please God. It is said that to simply recite the name of God with full concentration and heart will be sufficient to please God and release you from the bondage of ignorance and suffering.

One way I have learned to do this in Sai Baba's Ashram is by writing the names of God in a jotter, line by line, until the book is complete. I personally like to write or internally say something that honours an acknowledgement of my Guru as God. And I usually write: *Aum Sri Sai Ram,* again and again until I finish the jotter. *Ram* means God *Aum*, is the primordial sound of the Universe, and *Sri Sai*, specifically refers to Sai Baba. For me, this exercise acknowledges Sai Baba as the Universal and ongoing sound of God.

He says:

God has a million Names. Select any Name of His, any Name that appeals to you. Select any Form of His; every day when you awaken to the call of the brightening east, recite the Name, meditate on the Form; have the Name and Form, as your companion, guide and guardian throughout the toils of the waking hours. When you retire for the night, offer grateful homage to God in that Form with that Name, for being with you, by you, beside you, before you, behind you, all day long. If you stick to this discipline, you cannot falter or fail.

You can write any Name as a meditation, or internally say any Name you wish that you feel connects you more closely with God. You can say,

Jesus, I love You,
or
Dear God, be with me.

What is important is the language of your heart as you say your chosen Name.

Sai Baba often reminds us that God did not give us a tongue to talk idly or to hiss like a snake, or roar or growl like a wild animal. He tells us many times that we have been given our tongues to be able to say the Name of God! Truly, this is why we have been given our entire bodies, to honour God and be instruments of the Divine. Yet, we forget this all the time. These two apparently simple ways of meditating and being close with God can help us to remember. So, just do it!

The Pitfalls of Meditation
Introduction to the Kundalini

13

With all spiritual and psychic practices we run the risk of inflation of the ego. This was touched on in the preceding chapter on Service in Action. In meditational practices, the same kind of scenario can happen. The very thing the practices attempt to do is to help us to see the illusory nature of the world and of our sense of selves, but what can happen as we practice and become proficient is that we get a stronger false sense of self because of our proficiency!

The ego has a very clever way of being able to use anything to its own ends, even spirituality. I have seen and heard of people who like to demonstrate their abilities, and who not only make fools of themselves in the process but also give spirituality a bad name.

Usually when people first step on the spiritual-journey bus, they cannot stop talking about it. This is a particular syndrome that seems to have happened to just about everyone, including myself and it is something very difficult not to do. Let's call it, *The I Have to Tell You Syndrome.*

However, we do need to find compassion for ourselves here as well as for others. I suppose the main criteria to ask ourselves before we gush out what last happened to us in our meditation session is whether the recipients of the news are really interested to hear or not, and whether we would be frightening them or not. We need to consider that we might be putting them off forever from any idea of following the spiritual path! Here, there is lack of discrimination.

Then, there is the *Show-off Syndrome.* I think that anyone who has ever been to a public spiritual gathering will know what I mean. It is as though these people think that they have the go-ahead in this setting to demonstrate just how spiritual they are. I have seen some meditators go off into a supposed, trance-like bliss in very unsuitable circumstances, say, for example, at the tea break. I have seen others sway violently, moaning and groaning in a meditation group when the participants have been asked to remain still and silent. Here, there is inappropriateness.

Then there is *The I've done It Syndrome* which suggests that the spiritual journey is a holiday bus tour. There are people who say things like, "Oh yes, I've done Vipassana, and it was all right, but now I have gone on to do such and such etc..." Only later, do we discover that they sat for a couple of hours one night as a kind of introduction. Now, they think that they know it all and that's that. Here, there is lack of respect.

Then there is *The Grass Is Always Greener on the Other Side Syndrome*. I meet many people who Ooh and Aah at the latest technique they come across. Perhaps they hear of a particular prayer or way of meditation or a New Age course. They do it for a week or so, and then they are swayed by something else they read about or find in the next workshop they attend.

Of course they never get anywhere with this butterfly flitting about. The depth of understanding of their quest and of themselves remains limited. It is like when people flit from partner to partner when the initial honeymoon period wears off and a little bit of understanding, changing, and adapting is required. They do not want to do this and so go onto the next fling. Here, there is lack of constancy.

Inflation occurs when we are not prepared to sacrifice. When we think that we are on the road to gaining something all the time, or that there is even anything to gain. In this way, we always think that we could be missing something or not getting everything that we could possibly have. We cannot believe here that God has already given us everything possible to make our journey perfect for us. In effect, when we have inflation, we have no trust and we have surrendered nothing to God, we have given nothing to God. We are aware only of attempting to take and take. It is as if we are swallowing and swallowing but not digesting. And so we are always insatiably starved like the Hungry Ghosts of the Bardo Realm, unable to get any nourishment— in this case, Spirituality.

What does God want from us? Can God want anything from us when God owns everything that we have, even our very bodies? God wants our love. That is all we have that can be of any interest to God. God wants our hearts. When we give God our love, our hearts, in trust, it is because we know that everything we have is from God.

In this way, we can never fall into inflation. The ego can never claim victory.

The Kundalini

The word *Kundalini* is bandied about these days as though it is the latest new item that can be bought from your local spiritual supermarket. In the last few years I have heard many people glibly refer to It, obvious of what this Energy Phenomenon really is. And they certainly don't speak about It with respect.

For example, I have seen women experience menopausal hot flashes and dramatically express a version of: *Ooh, I just had a Kundalini experience.* Likewise, people exclaim in a confidential, yet loud enough way for everyone to hear them at their monthly spiritual social gathering, the equivalent of: Do *you know that my Kundalini came up last week?*

These are, of course, ridiculously extreme examples of the kind of ignorance that is prevalent in relation to the *Kundalini* but even though they can be funny, they are unfortunately true.

My own initial experience with *Kundalini* was personal and I gained an understanding through trial and error and a need for survival. I later came across books on the subject which verified my findings and then had a gamut of people who somehow came to me with similar problems and I was able to help them.

The *Kundalini* (Energy of Awakening Consciousness) can be activated through shock or through engaging in spiritual practices like meditation. But, this cannot happen unless a person is karmically ripe for it. And so, I have come to trust that when someone begins to experience this kind of energy shift it is absolutely appropriate and necessary for him or her to do so. For example, not everyone who is meditating regularly or who has had a shock will have any *Kundalini*-type of experience.

In my own case of *Kundalini* activation, it was the result of a tremendous shock when I was in my late twenties, a life-death situation, where I was stripped of just about everything I materially owned, and where I also experienced a huge emotional death. It would take another book to tell you the full story. Perhaps one day I will be able to write it.

As a child I had felt very close to God and God was the most important Being to me, but then when my wish to be taken *home* was never fulfilled, and I realised that I had to stay in this painful world, I became disillusioned. By the time I entered adolescence I did not want to even know about God. For many years I "went to sleep" in this way.

The *Kundalini* shock served as an awakener and it came in the form of a huge psychic and spiritual opening which took around three years to integrate. Don't think I got enlightened! It's just that I had been so deeply asleep that relatively speaking, the awakening was equal to my slumber. I have continued to experience intense shifts. This has been my way.

Initially, I did not know what was happening to me and I did not want whatever it was. It was so sudden that I awoke one morning to find that I could see auras, sense things and this was such an intrusion I could hardly bear it. I was working in a Government office at the time and my main concern was being able to go to work. As well as this, I could not sleep at night, was seeing visions, and receiving teachings that I did not want, and I was extremely sensitive. I did not want any of this... I remember that I said to myself many times, *I just want to be normal.* This was not to be, or at least not in the way I thought at the time!

Before I could really understand it all myself, and I was certainly not proficient, I was called upon to help others. Through trial and error and hard work, I managed to tame the fire, so that it could do its work without completely engulfing me. I was also able to help others to do the same thing. It was one of the most difficult times in my life, but, in retrospect, I am grateful for this Initiation.

So, what is the work of *Kundalini* and what is It? Reference to the Kundalini is noted as far back as 5,000 years ago, and It is mentioned in ancient Hindu Scriptures such as the *Panchastavi, Upanishads, Tantra Yoga,* and so on.

The word *Kundalini* comes from the Sanskrit word *kundal*, which means, "coil". It is symbolised as a serpent that, while resting and sleeping, lies coiled. The resemblance between a serpent and the *Kundalini* comes through the nature of Its movement, which is spiralling and serpent-like. *Kundalini* is the primal Cosmic Energy of the human body. This is the same Energy that pervades the whole Universe. *Kundalini* is thought of as The Mother of *Prana* (See section on the breath.) and represents the Divine Feminine Energy (Shakti) which is always trying to unify with Her Master, Cosmic Consciousness (Shiva). The sleeping serpent lays coiled in the Base or Root Chakra (The Muladhaṛa) generally thought of as being located at the base of the spine.

When the *Kundalini* is activated, the serpent awakens and begins to ascend towards the Crown Chakra (to complete Realisation of Consciousness) through the other six main Chakras, Cosmic Subtle Energy Centres of the body. The *Kundalini* ascends through a narrow passage in the spinal column and passes through these six psychic centres before It reaches Its final home of the seventh centre, the Crown Chakra. This centre is located in the cerebrum, the hollow space between the twin hemispheres of the brain. Where the fusion of *Kundalini* and the Chakra take place, the actions of the mind are completely suspended. Both hemispheres become calm, the inner dialogue stops, a person drops all sense of time, space and identifications. False notions of the phenomenal world melt away.

When the *Kundalini* rises, Its assent through each Chakra creates physical, emotional and spiritual shifts in a person, corresponding to the psychic qualities of the Chakra. For example, a person with a *Kundalini* activated Heart Chakra may experience, heart palpitations, emotional fears and a remembering of past traumas and grief. But, as this awakening purifies the Heart Chakra, the person will be able to access feelings of devotion, selflessness, and compassion, and self-confidence. It is in the time taken to integrate from one level of awareness to the other that problems can be encountered.

On the way towards the ultimate Realisation and home of the serpent, there can be months, most commonly years, of experiencing

Her movement through your psychic energy centres. And, in this, you can perhaps experience disturbances corresponding to the qualities of the particular Chakra as well as experiences of increasing consciousness, well being and even bliss.

You need to learn here how to be with the resultant turmoil, if present, and how to live in a balanced and happy way at the same time. You need to be able to identify what is happening to you and when, and to find the necessary boundaries. These boundaries need not be fixed but can be moved appropriately as time goes on. You need to learn how to be open, yet sensible, when, for example, to take a break, to have a rest, to do so called non-spiritual things, and when to stop spiritual practises, and when to continue. You need to realise that you are literally *playing with fire,* and you need to learn how to respect your matches and contain the flame so that it is neither extinguished or becomes rampant. You need to take responsibility for you.

Some of the Conditions and Practices which Can Activate the Kundalini

Shock
Meditation
Fasting
Reading spiritual books
Prayer
Seeing a Saint or Holy Person
Chanting
Karmic ripening
(Past-life merits from previous practices seeded in your being and which sprout suddenly with the right watering and conditions)
Becoming more inward
The realisation that there is a higher purpose to life
Withdrawal from satisfying the senses
Listening to spiritual music
Practising Yoga.

Possible Effects of Kundalini Activity

Energy rushes in the body
Crawling sensations in the body or head
As well as
Tingling, prickling, stinging
Feeling of intense heat or cold
Inability to sleep or need to sleep for long periods
Difficulties with eating
Palpitations
Pain in the body
For example,
Neck, back, along the spine
Emotional instability and outbursts
Mental confusion and memory difficulties
Hysteria
Madness
Sexual Disorders
Death
Sounds in the inner ear
Bliss
Creative outbursts
Increased awareness and understanding
Increased compassion and devotion
Enlightenment experiences
Increased sensitivity and psychic awareness
Psychic experiences
Such as
Seeing auras
Out-of-body experiences
Communication with spirit guides
Healing powers
Peace

You will most probably be aware as you read through these lists that many people must be going to their doctors with symptoms that cannot be resolved medically. The last thing they would expect, for example, to be related to an increasing spiritual opening is heart palpitations.

I personally had to receive medical treatment for two years from Tibetan doctors following an intense spiritual opening I had on a pilgrimage some years ago. The treatment strengthened my nervous system considerably and the doctors understood completely what had happened and what was happening to me. Unfortunately, orthodox medical training does not really equip doctors to be able to cope with these symptoms. But there are, of course, physicians such as Tibetan Buddhist, Ayurvedic and Homeopathic doctors and practitioners who can be helpful. I suggest that if you experience difficult physiological or emotional symptoms you seek these experts out as they can help you and they will not laugh at you. You may, of course, have a sympathetic doctor and if so get help from him or her.

If you experience any difficulties with extreme symptoms of either the positive or negative items on the list you need to take action. Most people have responsibilities like having a husband or wife, a job, a home to run and children to take care of. It is not necessarily a compassionate or spiritual thing to do, to go off on a wave of bliss for weeks, disappear and desert them all. Neither is it helpful if you become mad. This is why we need to take responsibility for our actions, spiritual as well as material and worldly.

I recommend people who become overwhelmed in any way to:

Stop meditating until one is balanced
Cease reading any spiritual books
or
Stop devotional practices which increase the unwanted feelings
Eat healthy protein and carbohydrate " heavy" food
And
Eat regularly
And
Often
Walk in nature

Hug trees
Clean the toilets
Do gardening
Paint landscapes
Sew
Knit
Play
and
even
Watch TV

These lists are not comprehensive but I am sure they make the essential point. Try not to be alone. Befriend people in the same boat as you. Find teachers who are experienced, who have had similar experiences themselves and who do not just have book knowledge. They can also guide you and support you when necessary. Be sensible. Trust God and know that even if you are not doing any practices to be closer to God, God is with you anyway. Trust in your responsibilities and appropriateness. You have been given them for a reason. Use your discrimination and vigilance. These are spiritual tools that will help you until you finally reach home. And remember, there is no need to hurry, for you cannot possibly miss out or be forgotten… There is wondrous Divine timing, so practice, enjoy, and be happy.

Part 3
Affirmations

Introduction

14

The reason I began writing this book was because of a promise I made to Sai Baba to do with the writing of affirmations. I made the promise before I really thought out any of the consequences. I heard myself say the words internally and was not even aware of the implications of my thoughts until later that day and after Swami had shown me that He had very clearly heard them within a few hours of my thinking them. I was set up — I had set myself in a *fait accompli*! And God, I realised, managed to finally catch me at the right moment, off guard, and was happy. For some reason this had to be and I had to write this book, but it was another seven months before I set out to make good on my promise.

This incident happened after I had been personally saying, writing and exploring affirmations for some time and using them in my work with people. I knew that affirmations were helpful. When people used them and worked with them these individuals usually seemed to find a change, a shift in their lives and attitudes. I found that they could be empowering, and that they could transform seemingly difficult situations into something positive. They could almost be magical. But were they a good spiritual tool, I wondered, and did God really approve?

And so, one afternoon in September 2001 in Puttapurti, just a couple of days before I was preparing to leave for the UK to facilitate some workshops and retreats, God played a little trick on me. I was thinking about the coming groups and about the idea of using affirmations in the workshops and whether affirmations and my thoughts on them and the way I used them was valid. This was in the form of an internal dialogue with Swami. I was the only one doing the talking and I was telling Him of my feelings, and asking Him, if He, as my Guru, approved. This was all happening as I was dressing and preparing to go to *Darshan*. Then, I found myself speaking out loud saying something like this:

...And Swami, if you feel that affirmations are a valid means of help for people at this time, please confirm this to me without any doubt. If you do this, I will even write about them...

A few hours later, when I recalled my thoughts and external words I was surprised myself at what they were, and how I had said them aloud. The idea of writing about affirmations had never occurred to me before. But immediately after speaking out loud to Swami, I forgot it. I left my room and hurried to the *Darshan* token line.

Now, in Prashanti Nilayam, Sai Baba has a wonderful way of organising the vast crowds who come to see Him. It is done through token lines. Thousands of people sit in orderly lines outside Sai Kulwant Hall, where *Darshan* takes place. The men sit on one side of the hall and the women on the other. The person, who synchronistically finds himself or herself at the front of each row of lines chooses the token (a small numbered plastic square) which will determine when their line will enter the hall. Those who enter first have token number one, thereafter token number two, and so on. In this way, there is no need to try to sit for hours before *Darshan* in order to be first inside the hall. Sometimes, it is the last people to arrive at the token lines who sit in the row that gets first token.

People usually want to get first token because this ensures a place near the carpet where Swami walks. If there is any possibility of Sai Baba taking a letter from a devotee, calling one for an interview, looking or smiling at one, it is enhanced by this proximity. But, for many devotees, the proximity is enough and it is elating to be able to be so near to Him. When there are rows and rows of people waiting in the lines it sometimes feels like winning the lottery when one gets number one, two or three. Sometimes, one hears excited and joyous cries from the *lucky winners* and they are immediately told to "Shush" by the *sevadals* (volunteers).

As I arrived at the ladies' forecourt just outside the hall, I was ushered to the front of a new token line and, to my trepidation, realised that I was placed in the position of choosing the token. There are around 100 women sitting in a row behind the one who chooses the token. All of them are wishing for a good number, and so it is a slightly unnerving thing to have to be the one to choose, the one that the rest of the women are pinning their hopes on. Usually, in these circumstances, I try to let my anxious thoughts drop and choose a token, surrendering the action to Swami, Whom I feel picks the tokens anyway.

The volunteer brought the token bag to me. As I placed my hand inside it, I heard an inner voice say:

I affirm I choose number one.

The affirmation was so simple, so clever, such a playful pun, and had so much the *handwriting* of Swami all over it, that I immediately giggled as I picked out two tokens sticking together. One of the tokens dropped back into the bag, and the one remaining in my hand was Number One!

I was the first to enter the Sai Kulwant Hall that afternoon. I sat right beside the carpet and waited for Swami to enter and walk along in front of me. I was delightfully reeling from the way Swami had picked the token. There was no doubt in my mind that He had done so. There was no doubt in my mind either that this was the confirmation I had asked from Him previously about affirmations, and that it was at His instigation that my mind formulated the affirmation. This was no coincidence. Swami entered the hall, and as though to place the icing on the cake for me, He also walked to where I sat and smilingly took my letter from me.

The happening demonstrated to me, not only Sai Baba's Divinity, His ability to read my mind, but also His approval of affirmations. I remembered what I had also voiced out loud and so I knew that I had to write about affirmations as well. This was a very clear and playful "Yes" to me from Swami. The result is this section of the book. Explaining, how affirmations can assist in healing the unity of our body, mind and soul, and help us to be happy.

A coincidence is merely a miracle in which God chooses to remain anonymous.

Sri Sathya Sai Baba

Why Affirmations?

15

We can use affirmations to help our minds be more peaceful, healthy, positive and happy. But remember always, that this is not the end of the story, only the beginning. All healing is a step towards Spiritual Wholeness. The end result of the experience of all our lifetimes is the final and ultimate unity with God. So, acquiring more peace, openness, joy and trust through making affirmations can be seen as a step towards this Wholeness and a helpful aid on our spiritual paths. In this way, affirmations can be used on a profoundly spiritual level for untangling the webs of confusion and threads of distrust and pain within us and for allowing us to be more open to our true birthright of Divinity and Oneness with God.

We live in an apparent world of opposites. There seem to be light and dark forces at work in our lives and in everybody else's. But, within the non-dualistic world, the home of the Divine, there is no positive or negative, no good or bad. There is only *Is.* (*Beingness*, a state of Being.) Spiritual techniques like meditation attempt to free us from the power of thoughts and their grip on the psyche. In meditation we practice seeing thoughts as mirrors of our illusions. We learn to not follow these thoughts.

If this is the case, then what is the point in making the effort to affirm positive thought? I internally asked this question and was given the intuitive reply :

As long as you think thoughts in this relative, dualistic reality, it is better for you to think positive thoughts, rather than negative thoughts.

When one thinks of this, it is of course true. It is preferable to think positive thoughts rather than negative thoughts because as long as we are identified with our thoughts they subconsciously, unconsciously and consciously affect us. Metaphorically, our mind is like a Divine garden. Its basic nature is heavenly but through time, bad habits and conditioning, poisonous weeds have grown where there were beautiful flowers and they have propagated so much that we can no longer even see the beauty of the design.

On the most fundamental level, our thoughts affect us. Thoughts make sounds. Sound is vibrational. Vibrations affect the way we feel and the way we relate to our world and the way the world relates to us. In this way our thoughts have a direct bearing on our health, our relationships and on all levels of our lives.

The power of thoughts is fuelled by emotion, by feelings. A thought with little or no emotional backing it is like a boat with no paddle. A thought packed with emotional intensity is like a speedboat with the most powerful engine.

As well as having conscious thoughts, we are influenced by unconscious and subconscious thoughts that also have a vibrational affect on our lives. These subtle vibrations are sometimes even more powerful than those we are consciously aware of and are the bases for the strong psychological patterning which we find ourselves in and which we enact again and again.

We can easily see here that sound, thoughts and words combined with intensity of *feeling* and *will*, make a potentially powerful spiritual force. This is why it is so important that we know and understand what our thoughts are and take responsibility for them. For, they also have the potential to affect us negatively, as much as they can effect us positively. But, if we *do* take responsibility and change our negative thoughts to positive thoughts, our attitude of mind changes. And, as a result, our health, happiness and ability to find peace increases.

Importantly, our thoughts and their vibrations are directly related to our spirituality and our relationship with God and with our own Divinity. On one level, when we have good thoughts, empowered by good feelings, good actions will follow. Sri Sathya Sai Baba and many other Masters repeat the Ancient Wisdom:

In order to achieve anything spiritually we must first make our thoughts pure. Pure thoughts lead to pure actions and a pure life.

As you can see, this is a fundamental Truth. If we walk around with a mind loaded with negative thoughts, how can any of our more spiritually inspired thoughts get a chance to be heard?

Many people feel that they have no relationship with God or that, at best, they have a difficult one. They experience feelings of anger, fear, helplessness, abandonment and unworthiness. I have met very few people in therapy sessions, healing sessions or groups who do not have some pain in their lives connected with their feelings about God. Their wounds enhance their feelings of being split from Divinity.

For example, this sore may manifest as a feeling that God has abandoned you, that God punishes you, or even that God does not exist. Importantly, this colours every other relationship you have. The way you feel your relationship is with God is, ultimately, the way you consciously and unconsciously expect the world and every being and every thing in it to relate to you. This expectation will realise itself and live itself out during this lifetime.

If, for instance, you feel that God has abandoned you, you will most probably suffer an experience of abandonment throughout your life and the people you meet and have relationships with will mirror this for you by abandoning you also in some way. *Or, you will abandon them.* This strong thought form has to fulfil itself, and especially so, when everything and everyone is God. Our feeling of being split from God, therefore, colours our entire life and is inherent in everything we experience.

This theme is played out, not only personally, but also collectively and societally. We have even *sanctified* this split, as though it should be holy. For example, the idea of *original sin* in the Bible is not only indicative of this split, but makes it religious. The story tells us that God cast Adam and Eve out of the Garden of Eden. People, particularly in the West, are unconsciously, subconsciously and consciously affected by this story. We are Archetypically programmed to feel that we are sinners and are not good enough for Eden, the beautiful garden of God, for the Divine Abode. This colours our spirituality, our communion and communication with God as well as every relationship we have. It is like pouring black ink into a beautiful clear glass of water. We spend the rest of our lives/lifetimes trying to find the clarity in something already tainted and from which we cannot drink without being poisoned.

I first realised the immensity of the effect of this *Archetypal original sin* when I came to the East and talked to the Tibetan Buddhist Rinpoches. I remember one evening at Rinpoche's study in Sikkim when he looked at me in a perplexed way, saying that Western people had such guilt and were always feeling that they were sinners. He told me how the Tibetan people did not have this concept, and it struck me just how conditioned and programmed we can be with our culture, traditions and society. He was at that time relatively new to the West, having only visited there once. This was one of the things that had struck him when talking to Western people and which he could, of course, see so clearly from his untainted newness to the scene! He saw, incredulously, that they thought that they were sinners and, consequently, they experienced feelings of guilt and unworthiness.

I noticed another aspect of this East-West cultural difference when I first visited a Hindu temple in the South of India. The Indian devotees wanted to touch everything sacred as though it was theirs: the idols, the altars, the bells, everything possible. The adults even lifted the children up so that they could do the same, and there was a clamouring and pushing which, to my then innocent and sedate eyes, seemed like a riot. I remember that when I saw this, my first instinct was to stop them and tell them that this was disrespectful. But, thankfully, I did not. I was confused, because this could not have happened in my church at home when I was a child. No such groping or touching would have been tolerated. At the Hindu temple the actions of the devotees made me uneasy because of my religious upbringing, I realised. But, fortunately I did not react. Later, I thought a lot about the meaning of it all because *the vision* had affected me so much.

I had been brought up as a Roman Catholic. But the idols and what they represented were far more distant and alienated from me than the Hindu temple idols were to the people there. This is what was revealed to me. The devotees at the Temple showed respect by prostrating, but they could also place their respect in a *form.* They could, for example, touch the feet of the Divinity and not just think about it. Anyway, their assumption seemed to be that:

This is our God, so why should we not touch God because God, belongs to us and we to God?

I realised, after contemplation on the subject, how much my conditioning and upbringing prohibited me from being intimate in my devotion with God. And, this prohibition also affected my inner connection to God.

Today, I value affirmations, not only because they are an intimate way of connecting with God, but also because they can cut through cultural and religious conditioning. More importantly, they can be used to destroy the seeds of the *original sin* in our minds. Any person from any religious or cultural background can affirm a positive thought in a manner that produces a positive result. And with a positive affirmation, any person can transform any inherent, personal, cultural and traditional negative or potentially spiritually damaging thought.

Affirmations *said with feeling and will* are like the Archangel Michael's Sword, they cut through all levels of our negative conditioning and habits, and therefore can profoundly heal our split with God. They help us on our journey towards Wholeness with the Divine. When we increasingly feel the unity of love with God, there can be no true pain.

About developing good feelings, Sai Baba says:

There is no death for the mind, though when the body is facing death, the mind thinks it is dying. The mind, it has been said, is the cause of one's bondage or liberation.

Bad thoughts beget bondage. Good thoughts lead to liberation. Hence, everyone should develop good thoughts and perform good deeds. Such good feelings can arise only out of Love.

The Wound and Affirmations

16

I find that each and every one of us has our own individual wound. And, that wound is very personal to us. It is unique to us, even though it may have some similarities with some other people's wounds. What makes one person suffer terribly might not be such a big deal for another. Sometimes this can even seem so alien that we have little empathy for the person who is in pain and grieving.

Why are they making such a fuss over this? You may have heard yourself say in disbelief. But the very next day you might be making the same fuss over something seemingly trivial to another person. For example, some people experience great suffering at the idea of being left alone. And, even in this aloneness, there are personal attributes which might make the suffering worse. The suffering will be dependent, say, on whether it is day or night or how long the duration is, and so on.

But, to another person, one who revels in being alone, *aloneness* may be just what he or she has been craving and yearning for. This person will therefore have little sympathy for someone who complains about getting a chance to be alone. The person who is craving solitude might say derisively something like,

Listen to her, she is having a wonderful opportunity to express her freedom and she is SO ungrateful!

There is, of course, no right or wrong here. How can we judge either? But, this is an example of how each of us has a particular way of looking at the world through our own thought patterning and personal preferences and conditioning. Because of this, our affirmations also need to be as personal, individual and unique as we are. Some impersonal, universal-type affirmations can be helpful for many. But, if we really wish to use affirmations to open up our positive possibilities, we need to make them as personal as we can.

It makes sense to realise that our personal wound will also be related to our feeling split from God, to our own version of the *original sin*. In their own way, both will converge and relate with each other as intense thoughts creating thought patterns that can become a myth, our very own personal myth incorporating our very own wound. This myth will most likely be lived out as a recurrent theme or pattern throughout one's life.

Examples of Myths

All my life I have been abandoned.
All my life I have been rejected.
All my life I have felt alone.
All my life I have found happiness
only for it to be taken away from me.
All my life I have never been allowed to be my own person.
All my life I have been ill.
All my life people have been unkind to me.
All my life I have had to struggle.
All my life I have been abused.
All my life I have felt unloved.

Of course, once we "buy into" these type of themes and believe them to be true, we collude with them and create our own myth of suffering. We empower this myth to happen, not only again and again in this life, but also, perhaps, for many lifetimes to come. Maybe, the myth you have now originated in a previous life. Personal Suffering Myths become a habit, an addiction to a certain way of being, thinking.

They are like seeds within us of weeds that are watered by life. They sprout and live their life while we ourselves die. But, we do not have to be a continual slave to these myths. Affirming the positive of that which creates our suffering dissolves the seed in us that sprouted a lie. *When this seed is destroyed, it cannot sprout again.*

So, in making an affirmation, find the negative, the wound, the psychic personification of your *original sin* — your personal split with God, and you are on your way to discovering what *you* need to affirm in order to heal *you*. This discovery can arise as a natural result of praying and meditation. I have witnessed this happening in working with people in this way.

For example, there is a golden thread of healing that connects Prayer, Meditation and Affirmation. If, say, you continue praying for a husband, it usually means that you feel alone, that you need a partner, someone to share your life with. It means that you feel that you cannot be happy without this addition to your life. If you feel alone all the time, this means you must also feel God is not there for you, or that God cannot help you, or even that God does not exist. So, examine what you continue to pray for, and it will contain the seeds of your split with God. Find these seeds and do not let them sprout again and again.

Usually, what we continue to pray for again and again reveals what we feel we lack. Contemplate on what your lack is. Rather than trying to immediately furnish yourself with what you feel will fill this emptiness, meditate, and allow yourself to delve deeply into the void you feel. And when you find what it is, affirm the opposite. For example, in the case above, where the woman wants a husband, she can affirm:

I affirm that I am at one with God.

Affirm the positive of the negative you find and you will have your ***Key Life Affirmation.*** Through prayer and meditation in this way we can access quite easily what we need to affirm as positive within us. The answer to your prayer lies within you. There is actually *nothing out there* that can really give you anything. You actually have everything within you that can make you happy and Whole. You have Divinity within you. You are Divinity. It is this Divinity which will also be your Healer. The result will be your *Key Life Affirmation.* It will not necessarily end up being the exclusive affirmation that you use, but it will be one that you will always remember. This will be the affirmation that will heal your wound and your split with the Divine.

I recommend always that people find and use their *Key Life Affirmation* and feel the benefits of this before going on to include any other affirmations. The point is that if you do not heal the fundamental split within you, then all other affirmations will not work that well. It will be as though you have a continual abscess that does not heal. The other affirmations, we can call them the *Lower Key Life Affirmations,* will only be as good as putting a temporary plaster on your wound. In a short time, the pus of the abscess will wet the plaster, and the plaster will fall off. This will happen repeatedly until you finally pay attention to the abscess, find the root cause of its manifestation and heal it.

Composing a Key Life Affirmation

Firstly, identify what you feel your personal myth is. Create a statement that shows this clearly. For example, if you feel that you have never received real love from anyone, your parents, siblings, teachers, friends, and that this is an ongoing theme of hurt in your life you can say that your myth is:

All my life I have been unloved.

So, now, you have identified the theme of your myth. This is a big step forward. The awareness of this alone is a breakthrough. When you then begin to work positively with it, there is tremendous on-going healing and transformation. What you need to do next is simply transform the negative statement into a positive statement:

All my life I have been unloved.

Transformed into a positive statement is:

I affirm that I am completely loved.

But, is this enough to heal also the split you have with Divinity that allows this myth to repeat and repeat itself in your life? The above affirmation, when repeated each day, will begin to heal your wound. But, although the above affirmation is a good and useful *spiritual bandage*, the process of your healing will take a long time, unless you ensure that you also destroy the seed of your wound fully. By healing also the feeling of your split with God, which is the reflection of the root of your myth, from where your myth originated, your wound will heal much more rapidly and fully. Here, is how you can do this. Take your positive statement/affirmation :

I affirm that I am completely loved.

And include the Divine, include the concept of your own true roots, of God, by saying something like this:

I affirm that I am completely loved by God,
in all aspects of my life and relationships.

Here, your wound is bandaged, and at the same time its original source is given Divine treatment.

A few years ago, during some meditation/inner contemplation, I experienced a profound shock when I realised, deep in my subconscious, I had hidden my fear of God. I realised that an aspect of me believed that God did not love me and that God, therefore, would not always care about me or look after me. Deep in my subconscious mind, I realised that I had an aspect of me that bought into the thought that God only cared for me sometimes, but not as equally as others. This I realised had coloured my entire life.

This shadowy belief, I recognised, coloured the way I accepted God's will for me. The way I had difficulty sometimes in surrendering to God, and the way I felt that God would be cruel and limit how much Divine and worldly love I could receive. This belief had limited the potential wonder and Divinity of my entire life. The resultant fear, anxiety and suspicion had also filtered into every relationship I had. Where I got this idea, I do not know. When I tried to understand it, I believed that I was born with this seed of doubt, and that in each life I have had since its conception it has found the opportunity to sprout and destroy my peace, happiness and the quality of Love I could experience with God.

The following affirmation is the result of my discovery. I affirmed the positive of the negative I found, and every day since I began repeating it, I feel less fearful and more strong and secure in God's love for me and my love for God. My subconscious split from Divinity surrounded me with a huge, unnecessary wall of defence that kept me in a prison of fear that isolated me and kept God on the outside. How could I let God into my heart when I could not fully trust God and God's motives?

My affirmation crumbled this wall. I have said my affirmation now for some time, and I feel that the words and their meaning are definitely an intrinsic part of my psyche. I continue to say it, not because I think that the seeds of the negativity are still there. They feel destroyed to me now. I say it because it makes me happy and gives me joy. My affirmation is:

I affirm that I have complete love, abundance, joy
and protection in my relationship with God,
and in all aspects of my life and being.

The Use of Open, Positive and Powerful Words

When affirming, do not limit yourself. Do not let your ego-mind minimise your potential. Do not say small-meaning words when you can say big-meaning words. I like to use strong and potent words like:

complete, fully, all, abundance, total joy, absolute love etc.

Why, for example, use the word *money* in your affirmation, when you can affirm *abundance*? Why affirm that you want someone to love you when you can affirm the whole Universe loving you? When you choose your words, therefore, try to choose those that have the most expansive and unlimited meaning.

Similarly, I like to use words that my unconscious and subconscious mind will

a) Listen to and hear.
and
b)That it cannot argue with.

There is a reason for this. The subconscious mind will take note of words but not necessarily negative words. Also, it will take and obey orders!

Jose Silva, in his book, *The Silva Mind Control Method*, writes how he discovered that when people entered into an Alpha State, (deep meditative state) their brains were more energetic. Also, he noted that when the brain was less active and at these lower frequencies it received and stored more information. Interestingly, he also discovered that when people *worked* on the Alpha Level they got in touch with Higher Intelligence. (I would call this Divinity or God.)

According to Silva, once in touch with Higher Intelligence these people could not create a problem. He found that this was a basic, all controlling law and concluded that you cannot, therefore, cause yourself or another harm.

I believe that affirmations work only when delivered from what Silva calls the Alpha State, and thus they could never harm you or another. This is important to know when doing affirmations. If something is not right with the affirmation for you, it will just not work. Another way that I describe the Alpha Level is *Heightened Deep Meditational Awareness*. It is that state where there are no unwanted thoughts getting in the way, where you feel fully present and where you feel relaxed and at peace.

If you make an affirmation, in the state of heightened but deep meditation, for example, *I am healthy and well*, your mind will believe you and will be convinced that what you say is true and will actualise your words into reality. Remember, however, that just as it probably took a long time for you to hold onto the *negative thought*, that it may take some time and repetition to replace it with the *positive thought*. Saying an affirmation once will most probably not work! Repeating it in a *heightened, deep meditational, awareness*, state could eradicate the seeds of your personal wound and myth for good.

Is it really that simple? Yes, but you also need to really believe that what you are saying is true, otherwise you are lying. A lie cannot be heard as truth. Why should your subconscious and unconscious mind believe something that you consciously do not believe? So, you need to:

1) Be convinced in the truth of your words.
   and
2) Evoke with full concentration, the words you are saying

Paramahansa Yogananda in *Scientific Healing Affirmations* says:

Thoughts have to be understood and applied rightly before they are effective. Ideas first enter man's mind in a crude or undigested form; they need to be assimilated by deep reflection. A thought without soul conviction behind it has no value. That is why persons who use affirmations without comprehending the truth on which they are based – man's inseverable unity with God – get poor results and complain that thoughts have no healing power.

Positive, Negative, and Time

For the same reasons that your mind cannot be receptive to affirmations that might harm you, I feel that the subconscious mind only recognises positive words. It does not recognise negative words. Also, it identifies with time in the *now* and not in the future or past. For example, an affirmation that would not be acknowledged by your subconscious mind is:

I affirm that I am not going to be abandoned anymore by God.

Your subconscious mind will NOT easily hear:

I am going to

Because in terms of the *now* what does this mean? It means nothing at all.

Also, your subconscious mind will NOT easily hear the:

Not and *Anymore* in the affirmation.

Therefore, what your subconscious mind would hear in the above affirmation is:

I affirm—I am—abandoned—by God.

This affirmation, therefore, would confirm your feeling of already being abandoned by God. You need to say the affirmation in the *NOW* and in the *Positive* as:

I affirm that I am totally held and cared for by God.

And know, with every cell of your being, that you are totally held and cared for by God.

As an experiment, try saying both affirmations and feel which one has the more power for you. Ascertain which one seems to register more clearly with you and which one resonates more easily with you. Which one could your thoughts mentally argue with and which one is the most decisive? Say:

I affirm that I am not going to be abandoned anymore by God.

Let this register for a few moments. And then say:

I affirm that I am totally held and cared for by God always.

I have tried this myself and when working with groups and the participants have always chosen the latter affirmation because it is in the *NOW,* it is *Positive* and it is *Concise.*

Finally, let us return to where we began and transform the negative statements of our myths at the beginning of our exercise to positive statements. Let us re-write our myths!

Re-Writing the Myths

All my life I have been abandoned.

becomes

I affirm that I am completely held and cared for by God and this is manifested in my entire life.

All my life I have been rejected.

becomes

I affirm that I am fully embraced and loved by the Divine and by all creation.

All my life I have felt alone.

becomes

I affirm that I am at one with God and my life is full and abundant on every level.

All my life I have found happiness only for it to be taken away from me.

becomes

I affirm that I have unlimited, unbounded and permanent happiness in my relationship with God and on all levels of my life and being.

All my life I have never been allowed to be my own person.

becomes

I affirm that my unique and beautiful individuality is fully loved and accepted by God and this is manifested in my entire life.

All my life I have been ill.

becomes

I affirm that I am fully loved and cared for by God and in this Love experience abundant health and well being

All my life, people have been unkind to me.

becomes

I affirm that I receive and experience complete Divine love, understanding and kindness on all levels of my life and being.

All my life I have had to struggle.

becomes

I affirm that I experience total loving ease in my relationship with God, and in all aspects of my life.

All my life I have been abused.

becomes

I affirm that I am loved by God and that this love is NOW tenderly showered on me on every level of my life and through every relationship.

All my life I have felt unloved.

becomes

I affirm that I am loved by God and by everything and everyone.

Reciting, Writing and Chanting Affirmations

17

I relax and cast aside all mental burdens,
allowing God to express through me
His perfect love, peace and wisdom.

Paramahansa Yogananda

Once we know how to formulate our affirmation, how do we go about expressing it? As we saw earlier, the subconscious mind will be much more receptive to us if we are in a meditational state of a deep, but heightened, awareness. The following are some ways in which we can say our affirmations:

Before the Close of Meditation

At the end of a period of meditation, we can internally recite our affirmation. At that point, our minds are usually in a highly relaxed and susceptible state. I recommend that you internally recite the affirmation 21 times with full concentration and the belief that what you are saying is true and *has already happened.* If *you* believe, or *your will* believes, that what you are affirming has already happened, then every aspect of your subconscious mind will believe it too and will behave as if it has happened. As previously mentioned in the section on chanting there is an esoteric, *magical* meaning when something sacred is repeated 21 times.

It is good to express your affirmation near the end of your meditation 21 times, two times a day, usually morning and evening. You can also do this for periods of 21 days. Review, and then begin again, if necessary.

After Waking and Before Going to Sleep

Another time when the subconscious mind is more available to conscious instruction is immediately after waking up in the morning or during the period just before sleep.

Again, one can repeat the affirmation internally or externally. If repeating externally, begin by speaking in a firm, clear and authoritative voice. There is no point in making an affirmation hesitatingly or uncertainly. If you do, no part of your body, mind or emotions will believe you or even notice you. Paramahansa Yogananda advocated that in saying affirmations, we repeat them out loud and then softly and more slowly, until the voice becomes a whisper. He says:

...Then gradually affirm it mentally only, without moving the tongue or the lips, until you feel that you have attained deep, unbroken concentration – not unconscious, but a profound continuity of uninterrupted thought.

If you continue with your mental affirmation, and go deeper still, you will feel a sense of increasing joy and peace. During the state of deep concentration, your affirmation will merge with the subconscious stream, to come back later reinforced with power to influence your conscious mind through the law of habit.

During the time that you experience ever increasing peace, your affirmation goes deeper, into the superconscious realm, to return later laden with unlimited power to influence your conscious mind and also fulfil your desires. Doubt not and you shall witness the miracle if this scientific faith.

Ritually Reciting Your Affirmation

Usually when I facilitate a group, I allow time before completion for a small but powerful ritual where the participants can compose and publicly recite their affirmations. This heightened and, for some people, exposing event makes a huge impact on the psyche. The mind with its complexes really listens and takes on board what is happening and what is being said because the lucidity of the event is so intense. Also, the psyche is evoked through the ritual. The affirmations are in this way empowered and not easily forgotten.

For example, participants are asked to compose their affirmations by writing them out on a piece of paper. Then we have a kind of trial run where each shares with the group. At this point, we check whether the affirmation is as clear, concise, and as positive as possible, and if it is in the *now*.

Then after a period of chanting, meditating and silence, each participant takes their turn, through the marking sound of a struck Tibetan bowl or bell. The participant stands, slowly walks over to a central table where a tray containing candles has been placed. The participant lights one of the candles from the central candle. While lighting the candle, the participant affirms to her/himself and all present their positive Truth.

The room is dim, lit only by candles. The silence is pregnant with anticipation and encouragement and the affirmation seems to echo on all levels of the group's being. Then, as slowly as in the beginning, the participant walks back to his or her place within the circle of the group and sits down.

Simple ritual can also be used when you are alone, and this can heighten the mind's receptivity. Ritual creates an enhanced awareness. But, I have found that it also protects the psyche from feeling too open or vulnerable by creating secure boundaries of ceremony, time and place which reassures one. I have noticed that when even the simplest ritual is used, such as the lighting of a candle, people can become relaxed and more open on outer and subtle levels. Whenever I use this small ceremony in individual sessions with people, especially when they are experiencing a lot of fear, they consciously and unconsciously begin to immediately relax and to let go as if they are suddenly being held and feeling quite safe.

Therefore, when alone, you can ritualise the reciting of your affirmation by lighting a candle and standing in front of it while speaking. Another way some people find helpful is to face the East in the morning or the West at sunset, or to stand ceremoniously looking out to a beautiful view, or up to the sky. There are many ways to make a personal ritual for your self and it can be a very joyous and celebratory thing to create and do. All this can enhance your positivity, strengthen your will, and empower your words.

Writing Your Affirmation

As we discovered in the chapter on Writing a Letter to God, writing takes effort and concentration. In writing out affirmations, one is not really saying the affirmation in the same kind of *heightened, deep, meditational awareness* that one can find oneself in during a meditation. However, in writing affirmations out, one is required to remain fully present, to be aware of what one is doing. And, the act of writing the affirmation and the containing ritual of the exercise makes a powerful statement that your subconscious mind cannot ignore. So, in my experience, the subconscious mind also really sits up here and takes notice of what we are affirming.

Again, using the magical repetition of the 21 times, I like to write the affirmations out 21 times. I do this for 21 days and then I offer the entire bundle to God on the 21st day and I ceremoniously burn the papers.

If I feel it necessary, I then start all over again and repeat until I feel there isn't a need to continue in this way. It is a bit like when we are feeling physically low and we purchase a tonic bottle. Because we want to feel better, we take some of the tonic every day as instructed and then one day we wonder why we are taking it anymore for we are feeling just fine. We feel that there is no need to continue and so we stop taking the tonic. Later, if we feel that we need to get another one, we repeat the health-giving formula.

I may use a variation of this theme by writing the affirmation once at the top of the page and then writing out a favourite mantra or prayer 21 times below it. For example, *Om Mani Padme Hum, Om Namah Shivaya* or *The Lord's Prayer*. Then I will recite the affirmation again and chant the mantra 21 times.

One way I like to do this, but which involves a little bit more time, is to write the affirmation out, followed by writing the mantra or prayer, 21 times. Then, I repeat by reciting the words of the affirmation and chanting the mantra or prayer, one by one, 21 times.

At the end of the 21 days and after the offering of the writing to God, it is good to burn the lot and scatter the ashes in, say, a park or a place to which you feel connected and which feels good to you.

Another way, is to buy a little writing book which you like and which you feel is especially beautiful or which you feel could honour your affirmations. Use this book only for your *Key Life Affirmation* and repeat writing your affirmation 21 times for 21 days for as long as you feel you need to.

Chanting Your Affirmation

Finally, you can chant your affirmation to a melody you feel evoked by. The sound of exquisite music reaches your heart in an instant. The action is like a laser cutting through all the mesh of arguing and disbelieving thought to the Truth and Peace of Your Heart. Once you connect with and remember your affirmation, and especially your *Key Life Affirmation* to a haunting and melodious piece of music, you will never forget it. Then, throughout your day, you can internally or externally chant your affirmation, hearing that music.

You can sing in Divine happiness
your Truth towards Wholeness.

Who Is the I ?
What's in a Name ?

18

Metaphorically speaking, I have found that people are not one person. There is no singular *I*. We appear to be unified, but we are not. For example, we have what we can call, "inner children" who are identified with certain ages and times of our childhood and history and with the specific names they were called. I discovered this in my own personal inner work and in that of the people who worked with me in therapy. I noticed that this could be such a strong imprinting that when something triggers a person into "that time of my life," they will react and even talk, say, like the three-year-old child who had the initial experience.

The *I* that we think of as *who we are* is comprised of thousands of what I call "little people" of all ages, likes, dislikes, attitudes and preferences, and complexes. So, when we say *I affirm*...I wondered which of these little people were listening. Also, which of these *little people* needed healing? What if, I thought, they all fundamentally needed healing before any further work could be done? And this is where I feel affirmations have tremendous healing potential. They can help make us Whole.

For a moment just think about how many roles you have played in your life. Think about how many different names people have called you that suited those identities. And, what about all the nicknames, or pet names you were given? Perhaps you even cringe now at the thought of them.

Most people in one lifetime will be daughter or son, mum or dad, auntie or uncle, Mrs. (sometimes quite a few times with different surnames) as well as Miss and Ms. Then there is Mr., Sir, darling, beloved, dear, sweetheart. If you have had many relationships, you may have been given many different terms of endearment or been called names that you did not wish for and which you would never like to hear repeated. However, they are all there in your subconscious and even though you have forgotten them your mind has not! Some of them may be basically positive, but others will be fundamentally negative, punishing and destroying. Affirmations can change little demons into little angels. These identities with nametags just need to hear the lessons, and they need to know that they are being addressed. The question is how to get their attention?

I experimented with this idea and wrote out all the names I have ever been known by. I realised that as I did this there was quite a resistance to remembering some of them.

Where there is resistance
there must be persistence.

Because of this resistance, I knew that I had discovered something important. The ego and its little playmates can be quite tricky. It likes its secret hideouts and when it gets exposed it feels very uncomfortable. I wrote my *Key Life Affirmation*, saying, *I* followed by all the names I had ever been known by; including all my childhood nicknames, followed by the affirmation. It totalled 13 names. I felt that this truly cut into my subconscious mind and there was no one there who could escape the command of the affirmation. I realised that if I merely said *I* some of these little people would just not listen, but when I called them by their name, they could not avoid hearing.

I have found that whenever I use this tool, and I use it particularly for the *Key Life Affirmation,* there is usually quite an initial, sometimes hostile response from people. Some people have been called terribly abusive names, and I have been moved to tears by hearing what a few have had to face being called. But, once the initial courage to invoke the names has been found, and these little people within us are given another message through affirmation, a message of love, a wonderful healing can occur.

I worked with a woman called Margaret who had been traumatised physically, mentally, emotionally and sexually as a child. She had been married three times, all marriages ending in divorce. Each of her husbands continued the childhood pattern of abuse, and they also called her abusive names as her mother and father had done. She was in her forties when we began working together.

Margaret refused to even think about the degrading names she had been called. But I encouraged her to try to recall them and eventually, in distress and tears, she managed to voice the horrible names and all the other nicknames she had been called.

Afterwards, we composed her *Key Life Affirmation.* She wrote the affirmation down with all the names, following *I,* and in as much of a chronological manner as she could remember. Margaret wrote the names down, (as I would advise you to do also) otherwise she might not remember them. There are usually a lot of names to remember and even with the best memory it can be difficult. In addition, with anything that we find painful to remember, she ran the risk of going unconscious on it.

I lit a candle in a simple ritual for Margaret to *hold the light* for her. Trembling and with her voice shaking, she managed to read out the affirmation. She repeated it again and again, until her voice became more confident. She continued and, as she did so, she became stronger before my eyes. Her affirmation had 30 names. It is not appropriate to repeat them all here but it went something like this:

I, Margaret, Ann, Mary, Anderson,
You Little Liar, Piece of Trash,
Ugly Duckling, Fatso,
Stupid Bitch,
affirm I am Love,
I am Divine,
and
I am loveable and beautiful
and
I am totally loved,
on all levels of my being.

She continued to recite her affirmation, using all the names she had been known by for the minimum, 21-day period. During this time, she said her affirmation 21 times, two times a day. At the end of the period, she knew she did not have to say the names again. It was time to let them go. They had been exorcised and she had been healed. All those names that were like hurt, wounded and insecure little people in her knew that they were affirmed as loveable and that they were loved. Margaret transformed and radiated peace, and from then on she said her affirmations, using *I* only.

You may not feel that you need to say your affirmation using all the names you have been known by. However, when there are names you begin to remember, that you find charged with emotion, then I would advise you to evoke them and allow them to fully hear what you are saying for 21 days. Thereafter, it is not necessary to continue using them and, in fact, I feel it is inadvisable.

Like all things, there is an appropriate time and timing for healing. To continue to use the names day in, day out, for months or years would, I feel, begin to concretise them. We do not want to set them in stone for all time. What is required is that we evoke them, exorcise them, heal them and lay them to rest. Then, continue affirming using *I*.

Lower Key Life Affirmations

19

I have named additional affirmations to the *Key Life Affirmation*, *Lower Key Life Affirmations*. I call them lower, not because they are less important, but because they are secondary to the *Key Life Affirmation* in terms of healing and making us Whole. Also, they are usually to do with our more worldly and exterior wishes and hopes, whilst the *Key Life Affirmation* is to do with our Wholeness, with Divinity on the most fundamental level. This does not mean that *Lower Key Life Affirmations* are less needed. For some people and, at certain times in all of our lives they are essential. But they are, however, not crucial to our Wholeness. Hence, the differentiation.

I recommend that you do not do them until you have done your *Key Life Affirmation* for 21 days, using all the names you have been known by. Thereafter, you can continue saying your *Key Life Affirmation,* using only *I* and also include a *Lower Key Life Affirmation* when you feel that you need to.

You can say more than one affirmation in any given period of time. I do recommend, however, that you use a maximum of three only at any given time period of, say, the 21 days and that this is inclusive of your *Key Life Affirmation.* If you use more than one affirmation, they need to be said at different times. There is no need to confuse the psyche any further than it is already!

For example, one affirmation can be said in the morning and another in the evening. As you go on in life saying your affirmations and you find that there is no need to say a particular *Lower Key Life Affirmation,* you may find that you then want to include another in your practice. There is ultimately no limit to how many different affirmations you might want to write or say in your life. Although, for the reasons I have already mentioned, I do recommend that you say your *Key Life Affirmation* always. You may find that you can add to your *Key Life Affirmation,* rather than making another separate one. This makes sense, anyway, as I have already shown the connection between the way our lives are played out and our own original split with God.

For instance, say that your *Key Life Affirmation* is:

I affirm that I am totally held and cared for by God,

but you are also concerned about the state of your health, and your relationships are difficult. In addition, because of the stresses and strains in your health and relationships, you never quite manage to do well in your work and so you are poor… So, here you can extend your *Key Life Affirmation* to include your present life difficulties. You can say:

I affirm that I am totally held and cared for by God
and in this love
I manifest well being, health and abundance
in my life and relationships.

The Dreams People Have—*Lower Key Life Affirmations*

In having people come to me, not only as a therapist but also as a psychic, I have found that most people want to know, to have and to hold, in as much abundance as possible four things in life. These are:

Love
Wealth
Health
Fame

The list is not necessarily in that order, but interestingly, only a small percentage would place God on the list. God is usually an afterthought. In the first few years that I worked with people, their suffering particularly evoked me. In my naivete, I used to think that if only God would give me three wishes, one of them would be to ask that everyone in the world would get what they most dreamt of having. Then, I deduced that they would find that this was not the answer, the means of their happiness–that something would still be missing and that they would realise that this was God. Then, they would be really happy.

I am not naïve now because I have since seen many people get what they wished for. What was apparent was that in this wishing, they also included God. They were so desperate they had to include God. But, once they got what they wanted, they usually just dropped God like a hot potato and happily went to sleep. I know people who, while they struggled through the most testing times, still found the time to meditate, pray, make affirmations, be charitable, and who thought about the implications of just about everything they did. I noticed that whatever it was that was lacking in their life that drove them so, when it was fulfilled, they just became contented with their own little world. They forgot about God completely. In fact, some became positively selfish and self-centred. I suppose that if things remain as good as they are for them, they will stay selfish and self-centred until they are dying, or have died.

Of course, when dying, it is usually different story. I have worked with dying people and have witnessed how they get angry at themselves and panic at the time they have wasted doing so much of what now seems irrelevant. They are panicking because they think that Judgement Day is about to happen, and they fear that God is going to punish them. It's a bit like trying to cram in study for your final school exams the night before, having done no work previously. Because they realise where they are going—to God, and This is the very Being that they have forgotten about for so long and ignored or actually Who they know very little about.

While they were content, they forgot all about the idea of Divinity and that whatever happiness they had was really only temporary or on loan. They forgot to have gratitude to their Benefactor, thought that it was all up to them, and that they would never die. What is sad, is that they did not know, do not know that God has never abandoned them, and that God's love has been with them throughout their lives, will be with them in every moment of their death and beyond.

Ironically, some people seem to get one or two of the desires on their list and find that the others elude them. Perversely, if they get one more thing, something that is all right in their lives begins to give them trouble. Some fortunate people seem to get three, but the fourth one teases their desire and never quite materialises. I remember a colloquial saying which registered in my mind as a child:

God gives with one hand and takes away with the other.

This was a saying that was going to mean a lot to me later in my life, personally, and in my work with people. My own mum also used to say things like:

Happy in love, then poor in money.

Another common one is:

Lucky at cards, unlucky at love.

There are many such sayings in every culture and community. I am sure that this is so because there is a relative truth to these sayings.

I asked God what this was all about, why was it that *nobody* got it all? I knew that this had to mean more than the obvious fact that psychics, therapists, priests and doctors are kept in constant work. The internal reply I received was:

If I give people everything they want, they will never want Me.

I realised that this was so sad, so poignant and yet so true. Actually, what it means is that we never want our True Selves. What it means is that we always want second best. And what it means it that we may fool ourselves into feeling satiated and content, like a little pig who has just had a hearty meal, but look at what we are really missing out on, in being like a pig. Actually, this ignorance is only another bad habit we have got into, but it is a strong one, that even Divinity can fall into:

The Power of Maya

There is a Hindu story of the God Vishnu who incarnates Himself as a sow in order to kill a demon called Hiranyaksha. But after killing the demon, the sow gets married and has lots of babies and becomes very content suckling them. The Gods in heaven try to entice Vishnu to leave the pig's body and come back to the celestial heavens, but Vishnu is so engrossed in the happiness of being the sow, that He does not hear them. The Gods have a meeting and it is decided that Shiva will get Vishnu back.

Shiva meets the sow, and asks her why she has forgotten who she really is. Vishnu replies, "Why? I am so happy here." At this moment Shiva strikes the pig with His trident and destroys the sow's body and Vishnu is freed to remember Who He is. Such is the power of the illusion of our world.

God truly loves us. If we are not contented like the sow, we should feel grateful. Shiva's trident is making sure that we can know who we really are. It makes sense doesn't it? It means that God loves us so much that we are not being allowed to go completely asleep on our True Selves, our Divinity.

Now, what has this all got to do with affirmations and our desire for love, health, wealth and fame? It is the same reason why I suggest that if you want to include affirmations in your life that you first find your *Key Life Affirmation.* Always include God first. Try never to forget God, and that way you will be in harmony with whatever else you ask for, desire and gain with your affirmations. You will have a better idea of knowing what it is that you really need and why. To remember God, is to remember your own Divinity. And your own Divinity, as your true healer, can only help and guide you, especially to avoid the temptation of believing that now you can have everything just because you know how to make an affirmation. But more on this, and the possible pitfalls involved in the next chapter!

In affirming for anything to do with *love, health, wealth and fame,* remember that it is unlikely that you can have it all. This is common sense. Look around and try to find someone who has it all in terms of our noted items. The people I have met, however, who do not need anything and who have everything they want are Saints and Holy People. This is something entirely different, and I have felt privileged to meet with them and discover their secret. Their secret is that they have ceased desiring anything but to know God. God is their constant companion, and they have, therefore, everything.

So, find your priorities. Look at your motivations. And decide what it is that you really need and want, and where you think God comes into your scheme of things. In this dualistic world where we find ourselves, there are times in our lives when it feels, and is even essential, that our ego-selves are soothed and comforted. It is essential in our lives that we are confident and that we are empowered and feel good and strong. There are times when the receiving of worldly boons actually help one's Divinity. There really are, I feel, no medals for suffering, for being a victim (in fact, it is the contrary), for being a whine, constantly anxious or miserable.

If we are happy, we are satisfied, and yet remember at the same time what the Truth is, we can be of great service to our families, friends and the world. The world needs happy, productive, self-confident, strong and capable people. It needs people who are happy to be here, and yet who have a purpose and who never forget the Truth, who *do not go completely to sleep*.

Just as we have to, Vishnu had to come to the world for a reason. In His case, He had to come to kill a demon. The only problem was when He got here and did what He was to do, He forgot what He had really come for, what this world was really all about, and He fell asleep. If this can happen to a God, imagine what we are up against. We also come into the world to kill the demons of lust, anger, hatred, pride, gluttony and all the other demons of our ego. But sometimes, like Vishnu, we forget and we fall under the spell of this illusionary world. We forget all about God, our own Divinity, and where we really came from.

So, we can affirm, we can use our discrimination, our will and our Divinity. But, always, we need to remember to have gratitude, gratitude, gratitude for everything that we have and hold already, and for our very God-given lives.

The following affirmations are examples of some *Lower Key Life Affirmations*, that I have heard, and which could be used in any given period of time along with the *Key Life Affirmation*. The wordings may be of help to you in finding your own words and affirmations.

Love

I affirm that my life is filled with love and loving relationships.
I affirm that I am embraced by love.
I affirm that I am with my perfect love.
I affirm that I am filled with love and am loved.
I affirm that I am happily married.
I affirm that I am free to love.

Wealth

I affirm that I have complete abundance in my life.
I affirm that I have wealth.
I affirm that I have everything I need.
I affirm that I am rich.
I affirm that I am paid well.
I affirm that I have complete abundance.

Health

I affirm that I have health.
I affirm that I am well.
I affirm that I am healthy and fit.
I affirm that I have a clean bill of health.
I affirm that I am physically, mentally and emotionally balanced and have complete well being.

Fame

I affirm that my books sell well.
I affirm that my work is always recognised and appreciated.
I affirm that I have charisma and that people listen to me.
I have complete self-confidence and assurance in everything I do – The world really listens to me.
I affirm that the whole world loves me and appreciates me.
I affirm that I enjoy my applause.
I affirm that I am happy making others happy.

The Pitfalls of Affirmations
The Potential Fall

20

He who acts offering all actions to
God and shaking off attachment remains
untouched by sin as the lotus leaf is untouched by water.

Bhagavad Gita

I have met people who have repeated affirmations and found they did not work. Of course, these people became disillusioned. I have also talked with others who found that affirmations worked so well for them that they became obsessed with the idea of what they could manifest by creating the correct combination of words. These power affirmers are deluded, they act as though life is one great big lucky bag and they have now got into the game of what to manifest next.

Meanwhile, these power affirmers also got disillusioned when their *luck* eventually ran out, as it had to do. Then there were other people I met who were so determined to have their wish, their will, at any cost, that they even became mad, mentally unbalanced, when it did not quite work out as they hoped.

So, what is the thing these instances have in common? Apart from the debate as to whether these people said their affirmations in the correct way, with enough belief and will and so on, there is, I believe, a fundamental Truth that we have to acknowledge and take on board. That is,

Everything is God's Will,

and we need to trust this Truth and surrender to it. The important point here is what we mean by this.

All of these people did not trust in God. If they did, they may have got upset when things did not happen as they desired, but they would not be disillusioned and they would not become obsessed with the idea that they know best. They all had an idea of how it should be for them, but they did not surrender to the final outcome, which is the TRUTH, the reality of what God has decreed for us.

Think about it. Think about sometime in your past, of at least five years ago, when you really, really, wanted something very much. Think about what lengths you might have gone to get it. Think about what you would have been willing to do for it. You may even have been willing to sell your soul for a little taste of it. Now, also think about how you might be glad that you did not get your wish. Think now, about how God really looked after you in not relenting to your pleas for help, in not succumbing in sympathy to your tremendous suffering and alleviating it by giving you what you wished for. Think about what receiving the object of your desire might have meant to you, and how it would have affected your entire life since. This is why whatever our affirmation, we have to *offer* it back to God for God's final say and recommendation. To put it another way, we have to offer back what we have designed with the help of our ego, to our very own Divinity:

Thy Will and not my will
and for the benefit of all concerned.

Now, on hearing this, some people might ask, "Well, what's the point of doing an affirmation, if I cannot make it *work,*" or "What is the point of even trying, if after all that hard work concentration and faith, I have to then hand *it over to God*?" There is every point. We have to make the effort. We have to believe that what we are doing is right. We have to *try*. We have to learn how to connect with our Divinity. We have to learn to be with our Divinity, to connect with God, for that is our birthright, that is our Divine power and we are entitled to it.

But, we have to know that as long as we are in this dualistic world with an egocentric personality that is determined to be the boss, who likes to take control, who likes to place veils of ignorance over our Divine Light, our Truth and Wisdom, we cannot always know, or be sure, whether we are asking for something that is goodness or not. In this set-up, how can we be certain that what we think we should have is Divinely right for us? How can we be sure that we know what is best for us? And then again, best for whom, the egocentric, the little naughty, or the spoilt child or wounded children? Only God knows who you really are, and so only God knows what is the most wise and appropriate for you, and for all the other people in the world who will be connected to every little step you take, those you know and those you will never even meet.

Thy will and not my will
and for the benefit of all concerned,

should be implicit in every word we say in our affirmation. We should have the wisdom of knowing that ultimately, the decision, the end result, the manifestation of our desires, our hopes, our declaration, rests in the True Wisdom and Heart of God.

If we do not do this, then we are no different from *black magicians* who attempt to have their will done, no matter what. We are here no different from Lucifer who had no humility, who thought that he did not need God. It is like selling our souls to have something that has been suggested to us by someone we might even know to be one of the most neurotic, and misguided, beings in the world, our very own egos!

I began to be aware of this potential fall from Truth, a fall from Grace, from Consciousness, in every step that we take, through the imagery and wisdom of a dream I had a few years ago:

Walking the Tightrope of Truth

I am walking a tightrope. To my right side below, the angels sit and to my left below, are the demons and the devils. I know that I have to be aware of every footstep I am taking, otherwise I can fall. I am aware that if I fall, it is not certain which side I will fall into. At this realisation, I am aware that I am trembling, sweating and that I have to find the calm and the courage to walk to the end of the wobbly tightrope. I have a wooden stick to hold in my hands and to help me balance, but I still need expertise and steadiness. It is the tightrope of walking one's Truth, Vigilance and Discrimination. If I can get to the other side, the platform at the end, I am able to stand in Truth. I am able to reach safety and God.

I realised that this dream was a thankful wake-up call. The imagery stays with me and sometimes is evoked in day-to-day situations I am faced with. We are all walking a tightrope, and we can easily fall into the angels' laps or into those of the demons. God is, I feel, with us in every step we take. God gives us the stick, the means to balance and to be able to cross to the other side.

But, we need to have Vigilance, Discrimination and Trust so that we can do this walk. In any case, we have to, for there is no real turning back. It is just as dangerous to turn back as it is to go forward. Where is the difference in danger in either going forward or backward on the tightrope of the dream? But, at least in attempting to go forward, we have the chance to reach God.

As we walk through life we are walking this tightrope. We are walking towards God. But, at any point we can fall. We need to trust that God is there always, that we can reach God, and we need to not even look down. There are angels and they will not harm us, but we have to know that there are also the demons of our minds waiting to lure us, unbalance us, so that we will topple and fall. Every decision we take is like this. How do we know which way we can fall? How can we understand? But if we keep our eyes on God, we will reach our destination.

When we make an affirmation, especially for the fulfilment of a desire or wish, we need to try our very best, look to God and trust that we will get everything we need, including the achievement of our aspiration—if the receiving of it will not deviate us and allow us to fall. In essence, this should be our most heartfelt wish, prayer and affirmation, that we will not fall, that we will remain in trust and surrender to God's will always, for the opposite is the road to hell. We could fall into a hell of our own making, of the ego's fabrication and the illusory world of pride.

Someone once asked George Washington Carver the secret of his success. He answered:

I pray as if everything depends on God
and
I work as if everything depends on me.

If we have this attitude of working together with God, we will succeed in our quest to be near God in everything that we do.

The ego will never surrender itself to God,
to Divinity.
or willingly lay at the feet
of its own True Self.

There is no choice for the ego.
The ego ultimately has to be squashed.
And God,
in God's own timing
will do just that.

The more the ego is squashed
the more Divinity reveals Itself,
in its continuous
surrendering
of Itself to Love
as it surrenders
and surrenders
and surrenders
Itself to Itself
to That which is Love.

21

The Power of Thought

There is an ancient Indian story that tells of the traveller who walks a great distance in the heat. By midday he cannot go any further and so rests under a large, great tree. He does not realise that this is more than just any old tree and is, in fact, the Wish-fulfilling tree, what the Indian people call the Kalapataru. The traveller tried to rest his feet and thought how wonderful it would be if he could have a bed to lie on. No sooner had he this thought, than he found himself on a luxurious soft bed. What a wonderful surprise he had.

Then he thought, if only a young beautiful girl could also come to me and press my aching, weary feet. Immediately, the girl appeared in answer to his longing and soothingly pressed his aching feet. What a joy, to find his thoughts so readily answered. He was amazed and he was beginning to enjoy this play. All I need now to completely fulfil me, he thought, is an ample meal, some delicious food and drink to take away my hunger.

Once again, there appeared in front of him an astounding banquet in instant response to his thought. The man, as you can imagine, was intoxicated with such comforts and answers to his thoughts. He lay down on the luxurious bed with his full stomach, in total contentment. As he began to doze, his mind had the passing thought, as minds do, what if a tiger appeared and suddenly attacked me?

Of course, just like before, no sooner had he the thought than the tiger appeared and killed him.

This story means that we are always near to God, represented in the story as the Divine, Wish-fulfilling tree, even though we might not be aware of how close we are. When we pray, meditate and affirm to the Divine, we are holding the trunk itself. We are shading our heads from the hot sun of life and we are resting from the daily journeys we have to make on every level of our existence and being. And here we can partake of three of the Divine Fruits of the Tree.

We need to remember that at all times our thoughts are powerful. When we are in such closeness with God as to share of the Divine Fruits, our thoughts are even more powerful still. God asks us to use our discrimination in our thoughts and also for our requests. We need to know that, like the traveller, we do not have the full picture, the full story or know how our wishes might end up. In addition, we have not yet mastered our thoughts. We are still practising on how to even control them. Like our traveller in the story, we are at times controlled by them and our desires.

When you *Pray, Meditate* and *Affirm*, resting under the protecting love of God, you can ask for anything. And, God has given you Divinity as God has also given you the potential to have everything Divine. So, the question is, how do you want to use this Divine and Wish-fulfilling Love of God and use Its mature seeds of Prayer, Meditation and Affirmation? What do you really want to gain from the tasting of these fruits? How much are you prepared to trust God, and how trusting can you be about yourself? How much are you prepared to trust your own Divinity, and how much are you prepared to trust and follow your thoughts?

On the journey through the proceeding chapters, we have looked at Three Divine and God-given Fruits. They will help you to feel closer to God and to include God in your daily life in a way that can make you feel happy and joyous. The offerings here are mere bites taken from these vast subjects. But, I hope that they have whetted your appetite for more.

We can never have enough of God. And, what is the most wonderful of all is that God never seems to tire of giving us more and more of what we need. We merely have to ask. These ways of *Prayer, Meditation* and *Affirmation* are three deliciously simple means of allowing ourselves to be closer to God and to let that Love flow to us more and more, so that we can be peaceful, happy and fulfilled.

Prayer, Meditation and Affirmation are entwined
with a golden thread of connection,
that runs through each one to the other.
The thread begins with our longing to be nearer to God.

And so we pray.
We grasp the thread further
and we contemplate and meditate on this nearness,
and we practice how to live in this way.

We grasp the golden thread even more
and we affirm what we find.
We affirm our Truth to every little part of us.
We instruct ourselves to remember that we are Divine.

We grasp the golden thread and tie it all around us
and we surrender everything that we have gained,
all that we have found, to that Divinity which we know is Us
and which is Everyone and Everything.
Garlanded in the golden thread of Light
we offer ourselves to God,
to the Divine,
in love
and for the benefit of all beings.

Om, Shanti, Shanti, Shanti.
Let there be
Peace, Peace, Peace.